MW00643663

EFFECTIVE EVANGELISM STRATEGY

AMONG FILIPINO IMMIGRANTS

EFFECTIVE EVANGELISM STRATEGY

AMONG FILIPINO IMMIGRANTS

DR. JAKE BOLOTANO

EQUIP PRESS

Colorado Springs

Effective Evangelism Strategy Among Filipino Immigrants
Copyright © 2023 Jake Bolotano

All rights reserved. No part of this publication may be reproduced, distributed, or transmitted in any form or by any means, without prior written permission.

Scripture quotations marked (ESV) are taken from The ESV® Bible (The Holy Bible, English Standard Version®) copyright © 2001 by Crossway, a publishing minis-try of Good News Publishers. ESV® Text Edition: 2011. The ESV® text has been reproduced in cooperation with and by permission of Good News Publishers.
Unauthorized reproduction of this publication is prohibited. Used by permission. All rights reserved.

Scripture quotations marked (KJV) are taken from the King James Bible. Accessed on Bible Gateway at www.BibleGateway.com.

Scripture quotations marked (NASB) are taken from the New American Standard Bible® (NASB), copyright © 1960, 1962, 1963, 1968, 1971, 1972, 1973, 1975, 1977, 1995 by The Lockman Foundation, www.Lockman.org. Used by permission.

Scripture quotations marked (NIV) are taken from the Holy Bible, New International Version. Copyright © 1973, 1978, 1984, 2011 by Biblica, Inc.® Used by permission. All rights reserved worldwide.

Scripture quotations marked (NKJV) are taken from the New King James Version®.
Copyright © 1982 by Thomas Nelson, Inc. Used by permission. All rights reserved.

Scripture quotations marked (NLT) are taken from the Holy Bible, New Living Translation, copyright © 1996, 2004, 2015 by Tyndale House Foundation. Used by permission of Tyndale House Publishers, Inc., Carol Stream, Illinois 60188. All rights reserved.

Scripture quotations marked (NRSV) are taken from the New Revised Standard Version Bible, copyright © 1989 the Division of Christian Education of the National

Scripture quotations taken from the Amplified® Bible (AMP), Copyright © 2015 by The Lockman Foundation Used by permission. www.Lockman.org

First Edition: 2023
Effective Evangelism Strategy Among Filipino Immigrants / Jake Bolotano
Paperback ISBN: 978-1-958585-29-0
eBook ISBN: 978-1-958585-30-6
Library of Congress Control Number: 2023904562

ENDORSEMENTS

Evangelism is more than words or good intentions; it is living out the Great Commission every day with people who need to hear the message of Jesus Christ. Dr. Jake Bolotano understands the necessity of taking evangelism from instruction into practice. You will enjoy Dr. Bolotano's pragmatic approach as he shares the necessity of evangelism in today's world, as well as his practice of evangelism among Filipino Americans with each reader.

Dr. Rick Christman

Interim President
Columbia International University

Pastor Jake has a heart to reach Filipinos for Christ. He has pastored a Filipino church in Columbia for many years while working full time and getting a master's degree and a doctorate. He recognized there was little written to help Filipino pastors effectively evangelize their own people, so he decided to write his dissertation with this in mind. This book contains much of what he learned and is putting into practice as he continues to reach out to Filipinos.

I recommend this book to anyone interested in learning what Jake is doing to further the kingdom of God as he personally evangelizes and disciples as well as encourages those in his church to do the same.

Dr. Brion Burns

Associate Dean, Student Life
Columbia International University

— TABLE OF CONTENTS —

CHAPTER 1

FILIPINO AMERICAN CHRISTIANITY

MEANING OF EVANGELISM

Before Jesus ascended to heaven, He commanded His disciples to "go and make disciples of all nations, baptizing them in the name of the Father and of the Son and of the Holy Spirit, and teaching them to obey everything I have commanded you" (Matt. 28:20). This "Great Commission" was given both for the disciples at that time and for all believers who have committed their lives to the lordship of Jesus.

For many Christians, the word *evangelism* means many different things and can be defined in many ways. *Evangelism* comes from the Greek word *euangelion*, which means "gospel" or "good news." In its simplest definition, evangelism is spreading the gospel, that is, the good news. Jesus commanded His apostles to go and make disciples and to teach them to do everything that He commanded them. The Gospel of Mark emphasizes euangelion: "After John was put in prison, Jesus went into Galilee, proclaiming the good news of God. 'The time has come,' he said. 'The kingdom of God has come near. Repent and believe the good news!'" (Mark 1:14–15).

EVANGELICAL

The term *evangelical* has a long and turbulent history, as reflected quite well in the literature on the subject. It's "a wide-reaching definitional 'canopy' that covers a diverse number of Protestant traditions, denominations, organizations, and churches."[1] Indeed, although the word *evangelist* appears only three times in the New Testament, "in the 1950s, 60s, and 70s, the name 'evangelical' was adopted and used widely by educated conservative Christians who affirmed the so-called 'fundamentals of the faith,' such as the deity of Christ, the authority of the Bible, and the importance of personal conversion."[2] When we think of the word, what comes to mind is the adherence of a believer to the authority of God's Word and the desire to conduct themselves in a community based on biblical principles and values.

Moreover, "evangelicals are a vibrant and diverse group, including believers found in many churches, denominations and nations."[3] The National Evangelical Association offers four statements to which a respondent agrees to be categorized as an evangelical: "(a) the Bible is the highest authority for what I believe. . . . (b) It is very important for me personally to encourage non-Christians to trust Jesus Christ as their Savior. . . . (c) Jesus Christ's death on the cross is the only sacrifice that could remove the penalty of my sin. . . . and (d) Only those who trust in Jesus Christ alone as their Savior receive God's free gift of eternal salvation."[4]

But being evangelical isn't just about telling the Word: "Evangelism is teaching the gospel with the aim to persuade."[5] The four major components of evangelism (teaching, gospel, aim, and persuade) mean heralding, proclaiming, and preaching. Evangelism involves a hope, a desire, and a goal. To persuade means to convince or to convert. Thus, "Evangelism is teaching (heralding, proclaiming, preaching) the gospel (the message from God that leads us to salvation) with the aim (hope, desire, goal) to persuade (convince, convert)."[6]

Evangelism is also "a call to service—to win people to Jesus is to win their allegiance to God's priorities. Evangelism, then, is calling people to mission."[7] The word asks us to reflect on God's sovereign power to redeem the lost and help Christians participate in bringing people to a saving knowledge of Christ. Evangelism requires action, not just thought.[8] In short, evangelism challenges Christians to actively share their faith with unbelievers.[9] It's all too easy for pastors to be so "caught up in church-related service that they have few or no non-Christian friends."[10]

I do not want this for myself. Instead, I want to live a life where I do more than talk about evangelism. I want my words to be backed up by lifestyle and action.[11]

The apostle Paul clearly teaches that "There is no one righteous, not even one; there is no one who understands; there is no one who seeks God" (Rom. 3:10–11). These words tell us that the world is in deep trouble and needs a Savior. It is clear that "the United Nations cannot stop the lawlessness in our world. Education cannot stop the lawlessness. All the armies in the world cannot stop the lawlessness in our society. Lawlessness demands evangelism in our world . . . [Thus] only the power of the gospel of our Lord Jesus Christ can stop the lawlessness of our world! Therefore, we must preach the gospel at all costs."[12] Put another way, "evangelism at its very heart is the natural response of believers and congregations in love with and on fire for Jesus Christ. Such joy and enthusiasm, when it is reflected in worship, is one of the most potent channels of evangelism."[13]

Now I want to thank Dave Earley and David Wheeler, who made a great contribution to understanding evangelism by clarifying what evangelism is not. They argue it is not choice, merely passing along information, a spiritual gift, just something you do, in competition with discipleship, based on your personality, the same as "mission," acting arrogant or superior, meant to silence by fear, nor a theological dilemma. Instead, they argue that evangelism should be a part of every believer's lifestyle. Christians, as followers of Jesus, should be evangelizing the way Jesus did. In other words, Jesus "literally became one of us and 'pitched the tent' of His life among us so He could get the message of God to us in a manner that was 'full of grace and truth.'"[14] Earley and Wheeler exhort all Christians to respond to the call of Christ to demonstrate a lifestyle of evangelism as Jesus did:

> As God personally brought the good news to mankind, so we are to "incarnate" Christ to the lost, that is, to penetrate, (pitch our tent) significantly into the lives of the non-Christians for the purpose of not only verbalizing the gospel but also to live it before them. As Christ lives His life through the believer, they see the "visible expression of the invisible God" as well as hearing the Word of Salvation.[15]

It's easy to see why such "a work of communication in which Christians make themselves mouthpieces for God's message of mercy to sinners,"[16] is unsettling to some Christians. Many do not feel comfortable sharing their faith, which is an "organic process of intentionally engaging individuals in their spiritual journey, joining the Holy Spirit, watching for where he is already at work to help these individuals take one step closer to God and new life in Christ, becoming the unique reflection of the image of Christ as the resurrected, glorified persons God intended."[17] Indeed, "success in evangelism is consistently taking the initiative, using the gifts and opportunities God gives us, to help individuals move one step closer to Christ" by demonstrating our faith through competence, character, showing concern, and wise conversation.[18]

Another challenge to successful evangelism "is the mistaken idea that no one is interested. We sometimes make the mistake of assuming people aren't particularly interested in spiritual truth . . . [yet] many people are tired of living without ultimate purpose. Many are actively searching for answers, as evidenced by surveys conducted by Gallup and others."[19]

As Jesus put it, "It is not the healthy who need a doctor, but the sick" (Matt. 9:12). It is clear that in this verse, Jesus was referring to those who do not believe in Him. The challenge regards how Christians are be able to establish trust among non-Christians because there are those who claim to be Christians, but their motives are only to take advantage of people. It is not a secret that there are Christians who are using the Bible only to exploit those who are emotionally and spiritually weak. Others use the church for personal financial gain.

Although challenging, Christians should not get discouraged and continue to reach out to their non-Christian friends and build authentic relationship. I believe that when Christians can establish relationships based on trust with non-Christians, sharing the gospel will come naturally. My wife and I, together with our two grown-up boys, went to the Asian market to buy food. While in the store, I overheard a couple talking in Tagalog (the main Filipino language). I immediately got their attention and introduced myself. I learned that they were new immigrants and had been in the US for two weeks. They also mentioned that they were happy to have new Filipino friends in America. Before leaving the store, I asked them if they were free on Sundays to attend church and to have lunch in our house after the service. Our friendship with the couple grew over the years, and they were grateful to have found true friends. We believe that our friendship with the couple was established on trust. Because of that, we were able to genuinely share the gospel with them and they received it sincerely.

In short, it's clear that the "word *evangelism* carries a lot of baggage, tradition, and emotion. Furthermore, most people have been poorly equipped with evangelism methods that are no longer effective in today's post-Christian world":

> The essence of evangelism is the message that Jesus Christ is Lord. Evangelism is our human effort of proclaiming this message—which necessarily involves using our human communication,

language, idioms, metaphors, stories, experiences, personality, emotions, context, culture, locatedness—and trusting and praying that God, in his sovereign will, will supernaturally use our human and natural means to effect his divine purposes. In a general sense, evangelism refers to our human efforts of proclaiming this message to any audience of believers and nonbelievers. In a narrower sense, evangelism refers to our human efforts of proclaiming this message to nonbelievers. But in both senses, we proclaim the gospel with the hope that our audience responds by trusting, repenting, and following and obeying Jesus.[20]

With so much meaning in the word *evangelism*, one must wonder who can then be an evangelist. Robert Coleman cautions us that the biggest problem of evangelistic programs nowadays is the lack of goals and right strategies. He suggests that Christians evaluate their strategies to see if they align with those of Jesus in bringing people back to God. Jesus begins by calling people to work alongside him. However, the people that Jesus wanted to be with him were passionate and willing to sacrifice for the cause: "They weren't the men you would expect to win the world for Jesus, but they were teachable. They had a yearning for God and the realities of His life." Also, "Having called his men, Jesus made it a practice to be with them." It's clear an effective evangelism strategy is anchored in the idea that after sharing the gospel, we should not immediately leave the new converts on their own, but we should spend time with them for discipleship and spiritual guidance.

Moreover, Coleman argues that another important lesson of evangelistic strategy based on the life of Jesus is teaching new converts about obedience. Believers should not only receive Jesus in order to become Christians but should be encouraged to obey God's commandment by sharing the gospel themselves. Finally, to be able to succeed in evangelism, Coleman challenges Christians to make plans for evangelism. He maintains, "Everyone has to live by some plan. The plan is the organizing principle around which the aim of life is carried out. . . . Every one of us then should be seeking some way to incorporate the wisdom of Jesus' strategy into our own preferred method of evangelism."

EVANGELISM: MY MANDATE

As a pastor in Columbia, South Carolina, I have a mandate to share the gospel, and as a Filipino immigrant myself, my congregation is clearly defined by the growing number of Filipino immigrants around me.[21] From a historical perspective, "migration from Philippines to the

United States began in the late nineteenth century and has been driven in large part by longstanding political, military, and educational ties between the two countries, including a decade-long period of US Colonization."[22] For the past fifty years, the share of US immigrants from the Philippines States has grown modestly from roughly 1 percent of the overall US foreign-born population in 1960 to more than 4 percent in 2011. In fact, "Filipinos now represent the fourth largest immigrant group in the United States by country of origin behind Mexico, China, and India."[23] Also, "the Filipino American Diaspora . . . is the second largest Asian American group after the Chinese Americans with a population of 3.4 million as reported in the 2010 census."[24]

According to Steven Raga, in the article "Intergenerational, Multiethnic, and Transnational Approaches to US Policy Advocacy for the Filipino American Community," there are nearly four million Filipino Americans living in the United States (Raga 2019, 38). The author adds that the population of Filipino Americans in the United States has doubled compared to an earlier decade. Similarly, John Burger, in his article entitled "Filipinos Prepare for 500th Anniversary of Receiving Christianity, but Also Reflect on Their Role in Evangelization," gives evidence that there are more and more Filipinos living in America. According to Burger, based on a report from "Inquirer," a local newspaper in the Philippines, North America hosts around 3.5 million Filipinos, while Canada hosts 721,000 (Burger 2019).

According to Luis Gallardo and Jeanne Batalova, "migration from Philippines to the United States began in the late nineteenth century and has been driven in large part by longstanding political, military, and educational ties between the two countries, including a decade-long period of US Colonization" (Gallardo and Batalova 2021).

It was clear to me from the beginning that most Filipinos in Columbia do not go to church or live spiritual lives. I know that sharing the gospel with these immigrants would lead them to see life from God's perspective and help them change their lifestyles for the better. Even more, I know it changes my life for the better as well. Indeed:

> Evangelism helps keep the gospel central in our lives and churches. . . . Evangelism deepens our understanding of the most fundamental truths of Scripture. . . . Properly motivated evangelism grows our love for God and neighbor. . . . Evangelism prompts unexpected questions and objections from non-Christians, which can deepen our faith. . . . Evangelism protects us from mistakenly assuming that those around us are saved. . . . Evangelism increases the likelihood

of being persecuted for the gospel, which leads to our growth.[25]

HOW TO SHARE GOSPEL WITH FILIPINO IMMIGRANTS

As a pastor of the Filipino American Friendship Ministry of Christ and having worked with the leadership of the Filipino American Association of Greater Columbia, I have organized events to welcome new teachers and nurses with their families. I have also attended the Fil-Am (Filipino-Americans) Annual Gala, where I've met new Filipino immigrants. Furthermore, I have been to many Filipino gatherings to celebrate birthdays, wedding anniversaries, house dedications, and weddings. During these events, I have seen with my own eyes the increasing number of Filipino immigrants coming to Columbia, South Carolina. Indeed, "in 2010, there were only 9,426 Filipinos living across the state. In 2019, that number grew to 13,333."[26]

With my active participation in welcoming new immigrants, I have learned that these immigrant families often come to the United States to work as nurses or teachers or by marrying an American citizen. I have noticed that many of these immigrants do not attend church nor care for their spiritual needs. Instead, they spend their free time partying, drinking alcohol, or looking for extra jobs so they can send more money back to the Philippines. As a Filipino immigrant pastor, I have a burden to reach out to these immigrants with the message of Christ.[27]

The motives for why we evangelize others is another important aspect of evangelism that every believer should understand. According to J.I. Packer, two motives should come to every believer's mind when doing evangelism. First, the motive to glorify God, which is the chief end of man. The author presents many Scriptures from the New Testament that clearly demonstrate that obedience to God's commandments brings glory to Him. He adds that "men glorify God by obeying His word and fulfilling his revealed will."[28] Second, every believer should have the motive of love for their neighbor and the desire to see fellow humans saved. According to Packer, "the wish to win the lost for Christ should be, and indeed is, the natural, spontaneous outflow of love in the heart of everyone who has been born again."[29]

The problem is how to effectively share the gospel with Filipino immigrants. It is true that "Asian Americans as a whole are less likely than Americans overall to believe in God and to pray on a daily basis, and a somewhat higher proportion of Asian Americans are unaffiliated with any religion (26 percent, compared with 19 percent of the general public)."[30]

Rather than using trial and error or following my

instincts, I decided to develop an evangelism strategy specifically suitable for the Filipino immigrants' context. This required research, and, in time, I realized my best approach would be qualitative—in the form of an illustrative case study. Rather than go by my experience alone, I wanted to hear about the current situation of Filipino immigrants in their own words—to help me identify their needs regarding evangelism and then develop an effective strategy to reach them.

For this case study, I interviewed seventeen Filipino immigrants. But it wasn't simply a matter of talking over coffee, tea, or my favorite, taho (Filipino sweet tofu).

MISSION

My talks with fellow Filipinos were situated in the context of my mission. A mission is an activity of the church as a response to God's call for every believer to actively participate in bringing the transforming power of God through the gospel locally, nationally, and globally. The word *mission* comes from a Latin word which means "to send." A "mission is thereby seen as a movement from God to the world; the church is viewed as an instrument for that mission."[31] The mission includes "the work of the church as being part of God's work. So, the church's mission is a subset of a larger whole mission that is both part of God's mission to the world and not the entirety of God's work in the world."[32] As such, the church should come together to bring change in the lives of people in the community. That said, the mission of God must fuel the church for mission work, as it "brings a correction to this view by putting God, not the church or denomination, at the centre of mission. Mission is the originator of the Church, not the other way round."[33] Put another way, "it is not the church that has a mission of salvation to fulfill in the world; it is the mission of the Son and the Spirit through the Father that includes the church.[34]"

Thus, a mission is not the mission of the church but the mission of God. In the words of John Mark Terry, six elements show the importance of theology in relation to missiology:

- Academic missiology must be seen vis-à-vis systematic theology.
- Mission relates to the missionary nature of God.
- Mission is the missionary nature of the Bible.
- Mission includes the missionary nature of the church.
- Mission involves the missionary nature of the Christian ministry.
- Mission relates to the missionary nature of the Holy Spirit.[35]

A mission has a threefold reality:

First, there is a message: mission assumes a distinct view of truth concerning the nature of God and nature of salvation. Second, mission involves the communication of both truth and a new way of life. Third, the purpose of mission is conversion. People accept the message, are integrated into the community of faith, and begin to practice a new way of life—a new life committed to following Jesus and sharing the truth about him with others.[36]

Another aspect of mission is about moving from one place to another. The book of Acts states that the Christian mission includes crossing borders and cultures. Before Jesus' ascension to heaven, He informed the disciples, "But you will receive power when the Holy Spirit comes on you; and you will be my witnesses in Jerusalem, and in all Judea and Samaria, and to the ends of the earth" (Acts 1:8). Another example of crossing borders and cultures is found in the Gospel of John. In chapter four, Jesus speaks to a Samaritan woman. In this scenario, Jesus created controversy, for it was not customary for Jews to interact with Samaritans, especially a Samaritan woman.

Another important aspect of mission that speaks directly to my goal of interviewing my fellow Filipino immigrants, is to gather relevant information or data about the people before beginning mission work. Having the right data will have an impact on the success of church mission. In short: "Data, used well, is transformative. Data is 'just data' until it is used to spur God's people to prayer and action."[37]

This is the reason why Jesus sends Christians to the world. And to understand the principle behind mission, we should look at the Great Commission:

> First, even if the entire Bible is essen-
> tially a missional book (and on one
> level, who would want to disagree with
> this assertion?), we would still do well
> to ground what we must do in mission
> on Scripture's explicit commands. . . .
> Second, it makes sense that we would
> look to the New Testament more than
> the Old for a theology of mission. . . .
> Third, it makes sense that we would
> look to Jesus for our missiological di-
> rective. . . . Fourth, the placement of
> the Great Commissions suggests their
> strategic importance. . . . Fifth, the Great
> Commissions seem to sum up many
> of the major themes of the Gospels.[38]

If we accept that a wider understanding of missions
does not focus merely on evangelism and discipleship but
also on social justice, which "for many Christians, social
justice encompasses from hunger relief to combatting
sex trafficking to reducing carbon emissions."[39] Thus,
Christians as agents of change for social justice can
concentrate on the "good news," rather than using the

Scriptures to shame others about their sins. The courage to bring up the topic of social justice is an eye opener for all Christians, missionaries, and pastors who seek God's wisdom to understand what Christian mission really looks like. As the Scripture said, "Learn to do right; seek justice. Defend the oppressed. Take up the cause of the fatherless; plead the case of the widow" (Isa. 1:17).

John Piper[40] shares the rich history of a church called Bethlehem and her passionate participation in world missions and expresses his gratitude to be a part of Bethlehem. He says, "To lead Bethlehem is to lead a global mission agency, not just a church. But a church that has become a worldwide missionary sending organization." Piper shares ten biblical convictions that drive Bethlehem in her commitment to global outreach: "(1) the fame of God's Name, (2) worship is the goal, (3) there is salvation in no one else, (4) God is committed to the nations, (5) the need is great, (6) missionaries must be sent well, (7) we live in wartime, (8) prayer is for mission, (9) suffering is in the plan, and (10) the mission cannot fail."

Moreover, Piper challenges believers to heed the call of mission. He argues that "worship is the goal and the fuel of missions: Missions exists because worship doesn't. "Missions" is our way of saying the joy of knowing Christ is not a private, or tribal, or national, or ethnic privilege."[41]

WHY MOST FILIPINO IMMIGRANTS DO NOT GO TO CHURCH NOR CARE FOR SPIRITUAL NEEDS

With this understanding of my personal mission, I knew the first step before I could be successful in spreading the gospel had to be understanding why most Filipino immigrants around me did not go to church nor care for their spiritual needs. I needed to hear, in their own words, what they considered Christianity to be. I needed to know which factors made them want to go to evangelical churches and which ones made them not want to go. And ultimately, I needed to know which actions of the Filipino church could invite participation on the part of unchurched Filipino immigrants.

NO EFFECTIVE EVANGELISM STRATEGY REACHING FILIPINO IMMIGRANTS

I had to start at the very beginning in this way because currently there is no effective evangelism strategy for reaching the lost Filipino immigrants in Columbia, South Carolina. My desire was to develop an evangelism strategy suitable for the Filipino immigrant context. I was aware of a growing number of Filipino immigrants in South Carolina. They are all looking for better economic conditions, and in that, they are typically successful. Thus, in my mission, I am trying to address not just

Filipino immigrants as individuals, but as a community.

I'm hopeful that my mission may contribute to community transformation. When a Christian clearly presents the gospel, it may influence the hearer's mindset and lifestyle, thus transforming their community. As the Bible says, "Dear friends, I urge you, as foreigners and exiles, to abstain from sinful desires, which wage war against your soul. Live such good lives among the pagans that, though they accuse you of doing wrong, they may see your good deeds and glorify God on the day he visits us" (1 Peter 2:11–12).

—— EVANGELISM AND DISCIPLESHIP IN —— THE FILIPINO AMERICAN CONTEXT

In different words, I'm addressing the Filipino *diaspora*, a word of Greek origin meaning "to sow over or scatter." However, "over the past decade or so . . . *diaspora* has become a term of self-identification among many varied groups who migrated or whose forbearers migrated from one place to another or to several other places."[42] For Filipino immigrants in the United States, their movements are due to poverty, suffering, and being marginalized. For them, "the very act of migration, of relocating to a new culture and society, introduces new possibilities and, by extension, potential for fundamental change. Freed from the rules of established cultural practice and the surveillance of family, kin and society, the migrant discovers that it is now possible to reinvent oneself."[43]

However, "as Filipinos migrated to the United States, Filipino Churches (and Filipino Catholics in Catholic churches) also started appearing where they lived. For Filipino Americans, church gatherings are more than just events for worshipping collectively as a spiritual body."[44]

The growing number of Filipinos living in America should cause Filipino American churches to be more intentional and creative in reaching out to the Filipinos with the gospel. Christianity is a mission for all cultures. Unfortunately, there are churches that have become so conservative that they do not accept any minorities. Although Asian American churches' attitudes toward others has led to the creation of a lively community online called Progressive Asian American Christians (PAAC),[45] which is definitely a positive, often, those coming from minority ethnic groups find it hard to blend in in a typical White American church due to issues involving language and cultural barriers.

—— MY POSITION AS AN IMMIGRANT —— QUALITATIVE APPROACH

So, again, I have been faced with the challenge of spreading the "good news" despite cultural difficulties. And again, the only way to move forward is to hear from the Filipino community by interviewing its individuals. Such qualitative analysis "is an approach for exploring and understanding the meaning individuals or groups ascribe to a social or human problem"[46] and "a situated activity that locates the observer in the world. Qualitative research consists of a set of interpretive, material practices that make the world visible."[47] It "attempts to gain insight into the specific meanings and behaviours experienced in certain social phenomena through the subjective experiences of the participants."[48] Sitting and talking with people, rather than having them fill out a questionnaire or some other method, also lets them tell their stories in detail, acknowledging their circumstances and inner experiences.[49]

Beyond using a qualitative analysis approach, I needed to address philosophical foundations, namely, epistemological assumptions that begin "with assessing where [the analysis] fits within the overall process of research, noting its importance as an element of research, and considering how to actively write it into a study."[50] The authors added that "philosophical assumptions are typically the first ideas in developing a study, but how they relate to the overall process of research remains a mystery."[51] This philosophy guided the direction of my research goals and outcomes, the scope of my training and research experience, and the basis of my evaluative criteria for research-related decisions.[52]

My goal here was simple, as "with the epistemological assumption, conducting a qualitative study means that researchers try to get as close as possible to the participants being studied," which means "knowledge will be known through the subjective experience of the people."[53] My goal was to spend real time with my potential congregation to get firsthand knowledge by immersing myself in their lives.

STRENGTHS AND WEAKNESSES OF THE STUDY

This careful approach to my methodology allowed me to gain direct information from my fellow Filipino immigrants in the context of their community. The case study approach provided the data needed to develop an effective evangelism strategy. Furthermore, the case study approach helps me know the participants' concept of Christianity. It also guided me to understand the Filipino immigrants' spiritual condition, the programs, and the activities that the church should be providing to address the Filipino immigrants' physical and spiritual needs.

But the major strength of my research comes directly from the interviews conducted with seventeen Filipino immigrants. The data gathered in this research are trustworthy and reliable because the data come directly from the participants.

I must acknowledge here that a weakness of this study is that I was only able to speak to seventeen participants. However, this is far and away beyond the work being done in the current literature. I like to think this is a step toward a great voice from Filipino immigrants for the general discussion of Christianity in the United States.

For this research, I assumed that if Filipino immigrants in South Carolina give their honest answers to the research questions, an effective evangelism strategy can be developed. I also assumed that during the research process, some interviewees might not give honest answers, while other interviewees might show unwillingness to participate. It is also possible that the interview questions given to the participants might not prompt enough relevant data for this study.

I acknowledged that even after the success of this study, there is no assurance that a Filipino church in Columbia, South Carolina, will be able to grow her membership. I assumed that a good evangelism strategy is not good enough if church members do not commit themselves to evangelism and discipleship. Lastly, I grant that the success of the research at hand cannot guarantee the transformation of individuals and communities.

However, such broad changes are not my mission. I am a pastor of the Filipino American Friendship Ministry of Christ in Columbia, South Carolina, seeking guidance about how to effectively share the gospel with Filipino immigrants. This church has been in existence for more than ten years. Although church membership is slowly growing, most of the church growth is the result of growing families rather than unbelievers coming to faith in Christ through evangelism. I hope that my work will greatly influence the church's current evangelism and discipleship efforts.

BRIEF OVERVIEW OF RECOMMENDATIONS

As such, I want to share what my fellow Filipino immigrants told me about their faith and about what they want in a vibrant, successful Christian community. We will talk about fellowship, community activities, prayer, spiritual support, and much more. I urge you to come with me on this journey into this diasporic community to see what they want from an interactive, faith-based leadership.

CHAPTER 2

MY ROLE

LEADERSHIP

What is leadership? This question may appear to be a simple one that anyone might answer. Some may say that leaders are those who are smart, skillful, knowledgeable, influential, wealthy, or those who possess a PhD. Others might argue that leaders are people with charisma.

As I was pursuing a doctor of ministerial leadership degree and seeking to develop an effective evangelism strategy for Filipino immigrants in Columbia, South Carolina, I was seeking a model of leadership. I was strongly convinced that no one can claim to have reached the pinnacle of leadership or can boast about becoming a great leader overnight. So, I defined "leadership" as the ability to influence others through trust and confidence so that together they can achieve common goals. Leaders should continue to develop themselves to become effective leaders as they set the vision, engage people, and execute goals.

I researched the term and found many definitions of leaders in various role, such as leaders of corporation and leaders in relationships. After considering these different views of leadership, I found three words that form a common thread: ability, relationship, and goal. Leadership is not just about exercising certain abilities, or building relationship through a charismatic personality or because there is a goal to achieve. An effective leader should inspire trust and confidence.

In particular, I'm interested in what is called "servant leadership," which "begins with the natural feeling that one wants to serve, to serve first. Then conscious choice brings one to aspire to lead."[54] Of course, the personification of a servant leader is found in Jesus Christ. The Bible teaches us that in the upper room, after Jesus and the disciples had eaten supper, Jesus wrapped a towel around his waist and began to wash the disciple's feet (John 13:1–17). Thus, Jesus' style of leadership demonstrated servanthood. Later, although the apostles were known to have been with Jesus, and they were able—with God's help—to drive out demonic forces in the power and authority of Jesus, and they had seen a great demonstration of Jesus' power through healing and miracles, they remained servants and did not use their influence for personal gain.

Elsewhere in the New Testament, James and John, the sons of Zebedee, came to Jesus and made a request to sit at Jesus' right side and left side in his glory. Jesus' reply still challenges leaders today. He said, "Not so with you. Instead, whoever wants to become great among you must be your servant, and whoever wants to be first must be slave of all. For even the Son of Man did not come to be served, but to serve, and to give his life as a ransom for many" (Mark 10:43–45).

I have been blessed to serve in the ministry for twenty years, acting in different capacities such as group leader, associate pastor, and eventually lead pastor. During that time, I have noticed only one style of leadership that always comes naturally: servant leadership. It is the most effective way to lead others because it teaches people how to think about others' well-being and personal growth.

According to servant leadership theory, a researcher is no greater than anyone else and is not the only person in an organization who possesses great leadership qualities. I was also reminded that I am not the only person in an organization responsible for bringing about change and success. Thus, servant leadership turns the focus onto meeting the needs of others through personal service and commitment.

Effective leadership is needed for an effective evangelism strategy for Filipino immigrants in my city of Columbia, which started with the gaining the leadership skills necessary to gather data and move from my role as an evangelist to my role as a disciple.

DISCIPLESHIP

Discipleship is the believer's call to help others grow physically and spiritually to become like Christ. To act as a disciple is to deliberately do something good for someone so that they will become like Christ in the pro-cess. So, before a person can make a disciple, they must first become a disciple. So, "being a disciple of Christ, in other words, does not begin with something we do. It begins with something Christ did."[55]

I look to Garrett Kello, who offers the following char-acteristics of a disciple:

- Disciples follow Jesus.
- Disciples imitate and replicate Jesus.
- Disciples help others follow Jesus.
- Disciples intentionally build relationships.
- Disciples depend upon grace.[56]

For Christians, grace is understood as receiving something from God that we do not deserve. However, Scripture makes it clear that grace is more than just re-ceiving what we do not deserve, as grace points us to the very presence of God in us. Scripture says, "For the grace of God has been revealed, bringing salvation to all peo-ple" (Titus 2:11). Grace, therefore, is the very presence of God who came to seek and to save those who are lost (Luke 19:10). Furthermore, the apostle Paul made men-tion that the salvation of mankind was made possible by God's grace (Eph. 2:8–9).

Paul, who wrote thirteen out of twenty-seven books in the New Testament, testified how he experienced grace. Acts 9:1–19 records the narrative of Paul's personal experience of grace. While he was on the way to destroy Christianity, the Lord met him on the road to Damascus, where grace appeared and made him the bearer of grace to the gentiles (Acts 9:15). The same story that echoes when John Newton, who was in slave trading business, had encountered grace in the middle of the storm and later penned the famous hymn "Amazing Grace." Where the first stanza *says, "Amazing grace, how sweet the sound, that saved a wretch like me. I once was lost, but now am found. Was blind, but now I see."* Grace has set us free and made us right in the eyes of God (Rom. 3:24).

We must consider two questions: who is a disciple, and what are the conditions of being a disciple? As Christians, pastors, and missionaries, we are challenged to become successful in transforming discipleship. We should consider living lives that are not centered on materialism, that demonstrate genuine love for God, and being people who deny ourselves and carry our own crosses, and who show a willingness to abandon everything for God.[57] If we as Christians do not grasp the real meaning of discipleship, it leads only to thinking of methods and techniques. The danger is that Christians focus more on the activities rather than on Christ.[58]

Moreover, when we talk about discipleship, we cannot separate suffering as a part of the process of becoming like Jesus. Suffering is a clear actualization of becoming a disciple of Christ. One thinks of C.S. Lewis's personal struggles as a disciple of Christ. He wrote in 1950, "My Dear George, I shall be completely alone at the Kilns . . . from Aug 11 to Aug 19th and am like to fall into a whoreson melancholy."[59] Lewis's struggles were mentioned in his sermon preached on January 29, 1956:

> I come into the presence of God with a great fear lest anything should happen to me within that presence which will prove too intolerably inconvenient when I have come out again into 'ordinary' life. I don't want to be carried away into any resolution which I shall afterwards regret. For I know I shall be feeling quite different after breakfast; I don't want anything to happen to me at the altar which will run up too big a bill to pay then.[60]

Suffering for being a disciple of Jesus should not be a strange issue. The Bible made it clear that to become a disciple of Jesus entails persecution. Jesus said, "Remember what I told you: 'A servant is not greater than his master.' If they persecuted me, they will persecute you also" (John 15:20a). Again, Jesus said, "You will be hated by everyone because of me, but the one who stands firm to the end will be saved" (Matt. 10:22).

Another passage of Scripture that clearly shows suffering as part of becoming a disciple of Christ is in 2 Corinthians. Here, Paul described his personal struggles as a disciple, writing:

> Are they servants of Christ? (I am out of my mind to talk like this.) I am more. I have worked much harder, been in prison more frequently, been flogged more severely, and been exposed to death again and again. Five times I received from the Jews the forty lashes minus one. Three times I was beaten with rods, once I was pelted with stones, three times I was shipwrecked, I spent a night and a day in the open sea, I have been constantly on the move. I have been in danger from rivers, in danger from bandits, in danger from my fellow Jews, in danger from Gentiles; in danger in the city, in danger in the country, in danger at sea; and in danger from false believers. I have labored and toiled and have often gone without sleep; I have known hunger and thirst and have often gone without food; I have been cold and naked. (2 Cor. 11:23–27)

Though discipleship comes with struggles, those struggles are about becoming more Christlike. Indeed, "true Christian discipleship, Lewis would have us understand, is first a matter of the heart—the inner life: the recognition, acceptance, and surrender to God's absolute authority over all the affairs of one's life in a way that leaves no place to which one may call one's own."[61]

Adam J. Copeland argues that following Jesus is a call to leadership. Leadership is not just about leading someone for the sake of leadership, but discipleship is a kind of leadership that results in a life being transformed. His words are most needed today especially for those who are practicing discipleship and for all Christians whose hearts are being turned to disciple others. Copeland stresses that the world needs Christian leaders who are passionate for the gospel and willing to sacrifice for the kingdom. He argues, "We need leaders with a passion for the gospel, with Bibles that are worn, with ears to hear and with communities to support them. We need leaders drawn to the work of building God's kingdom instead of building their résumés. We need leaders with admirable ethics and deep faith foundations. We need leaders who follow."[62]

We must that being a disciple is deliberately doing something good for someone so that they will become like Christ in the process. Before a person can make a disciple, they must first become a disciple. Indeed, "being a disciple of Christ, in other words does not begin with something we do. It begins with something Christ did."[63] As for discipleship, the author contended that "our discipleship to Christ begins when we hear those two words and obey them: 'Follow me.'"

In other words, I needed to be a disciple for my fellow Filipino immigrants, which meant living a life as an example and reaching out.

——— THE ROLE OF SOCIAL MEDIA IN ——— EVANGELISM AND DISCIPLESHIP

To reach out, obviously, I employed the power of social media as a tool to bring the gospel to the hearts of Filipino immigrants in Columbia.[64] In that, I took advantage of how "social media, including Facebook, Twitter, Instagram, and a multitude of newer networks that may or may not become household names, have an enormous impact on modern culture, especially on Millennials and Generation Y . . . [the] smartphone has created a world where most people are never a few inches, taps, and swipes away from finding out what other people are thinking and saying about them."[65] However, I was also cautious about social media's "cancel culture" and other means of causing separation among people.

In a world where social media is all around us, it is high time that the church should determine the scope and limitation of social media in evangelism and discipleship. We cannot deny that social media is one of the most effective platforms to convey the gospel message. Therefore, we should ask how we can use social media as a tool to help the church in her evangelism and discipleship program.

Many scholars have weighed in on this issue. Lara Williams stresses that according to the annual Edelman Trust Barometer survey, only one out of four Britons trust social media.[66] Williams believes these people are right, particularly regarding Facebook. Williams noted that 76 percent of adults in the United Kingdom use social media and, "many spend around three hours a day and believe that spending this much time on platforms can only make people more miserable." Moreover, Williams is convinced that social media is addictive and draws people away from faith. Meanwhile, Nadeem Badshah notes that "faith groups have supported the Church of England's first-ever digital commandments to combat abuse and fake news on social media."[67] Badshah argues that although social media can be an effective tool to spread the Hindu faith, there are also instances when social media is being used to spread hatred and lies. He adds that "social media has transformed the way we live our lives. Each time we interact online, we have the opportunity either to add to currents of cynicism and abuse, or to choose instead to share light and grace." Meanwhile, Paul C. MacClure agrees that social media is a tool that can build up or destroy a person. MacClure argues that "despite their usefulness and popularity, these new technologies can produce unintended consequences."[68] And Roxane Salonen contends that "many Catholics—including parents, kids, and clergy—find that social media has become an essential component of their faith lives, and they're willing to put up with the pitfalls to utilize the positives."[69]

Social media can be a great tool for evangelism and discipleship, and the church should stand against the misuse and abuse of social media. The church should use all its power and authority to educate both young people and adults in the church about how to use social media in a way that honors the Lord.

CHAPTER 3:

TALKING TO FELLOW FILIPINOS ABOUT CHRIST

DECIDING ON A CASE STUDY

Being faced with my mission to be a disciple to my fellow Filipino immigrants in Columbia, I noticed that many of these immigrants do not attend church nor care for their spiritual needs. To reach out to them, I needed to know more than my own perspective. I needed to gather data relevant to developing an evangelism strategy for Filipino immigrants in South Carolina.

I need to note that my research was conducted during the lockdowns of the COVID-19 pandemic, which had a profound and global impact. Some Filipino immigrants who may have participated under normal circumstances chose not to participate in light of the health concerns of the pandemic. However, their nonparticipation did not negate my ability to gather the data needed for this research.

TALKING TO MY FELLOWS
FACE-TO-FACE

I interviewed seventeen Filipino immigrants from three different generations: young adults, eighteen to thirty years old; middle-aged, thirty-one to fifty; and elderly, fifty-one and older. Other criteria included their length of stay in the United States, their English proficiency, and the Filipino dialects they spoke.

I have met many Filipino Americans in the community who fall into these three categories through events like Christmas celebrations, birthday parties, and social gatherings. I contacted these people through text messages and Facebook messenger, inviting them to participate in this study.[70]

SELECTION OF PARTICIPANTS

The first step in selecting participants for this study involved identifying twenty Filipino immigrants in Columbia, and ultimately, I was able to speak with seventeen of them, six of whom were female and eleven males. Here's a quick look at my interviewees.[71]

PARTICIPANTS	YEARS IN THE US	LANGUAGE/DIALECTS
Ruben – Male, Elderly	67	English, Tagalog
Marie– Female, Middle aged	17	English, Tagalog
Edward – Male, Young adults	15	English, Tagalog, Ilocano
George– Male, Young adults	15	English, Tagalog, Hiligaynon
Randy – Male, Young adults	14	English, Tagalog, Visayan, Hiligaynon
Albert – Male, Young adults	15	English, Tagalog
Donna – Female, Middle aged	10	English, Tagalog
Tess – Female, Middle aged	16	English, Tagalog, Visayan
Caleb – Male, Middle aged	8	English, Tagalog
Danny– Male, Elderly	15	English, Tagalog, Ilocano
Isabel– Female, Middle aged	8	English, Tagalog
Robert – Male, Middle aged	15	English Tagalog
Alma – Female, Middle aged	1.7	English, Tagalog, Visayan
Renato – Male, Middle aged	1.5	English, Tagalog, Visayan
Lorna– Female, Elderly	9	English, Tagalog, Kapampangan
Rudy – Male, Middle aged	29	English, Visayan
Francis – Male, Elderly	48	English, Tagalog, Visayan

(Table 1)

Having three different age groups increased the validity and the reliability of this research.

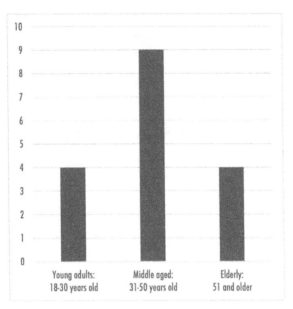

(Chart 1)

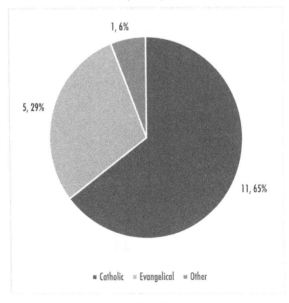

■ Catholic ⬚ Evangelical ⬚ Other

(Chart 2)

The interviews with the Filipino immigrants revealed that eleven (65%) of the participants were practicing Roman Catholicism. Five (29%) of the participants were involved in an evangelical church, and one (6%) participant had never been in any church.[72]

During the interviews, I asked the participants to elaborate on their answers and add clarification to help me better understand their responses. Interviews were conducted at a time that was convenient to the participants at a neutral location free from the distractions of the participant's home. To keep things as above board as possible, I did not conduct interviews when the participants were alone. Each participant was asked open-ended questions, and interviews lasted from fifteen to twenty minutes.

The following interview questions were asked during each interview:[73]

a. What did you learn about Christianity while you were in the Philippines?

b. What have you learned about Christianity while living in the United States?

c. How does Christianity compare to other religions?

d. In your understanding, how would you describe Christianity?

e. What do you think other Filipino immigrants would say about Christianity?

f. What questions do you have about Christianity?

g. In your experience, what has drawn you to attend a church gathering?

h. Have people you know who attend a church been a factor in your decision to attend church gatherings? If so, in what ways?

i. In your experience, what has kept you from attending church gatherings?

j. Have people you know who attend a church been a factor in your decision not to attend church gatherings? If so, in what ways?

k. What could a church do to make it more inviting for you to attend?

l. What activities could a church provide that would prompt you to consider attending?

m. What could a church provide that would help you in your daily life?

I also contacted five participants through text messages and Facebook messenger to see if I could visit them for further clarification and to give the participants time to ask any questions about the study. Two of the observations took place after conducting the interview. I wanted to understand the Filipino immigrants' religious beliefs, their concepts about Christianity, and how they conduct their lives based on their religious beliefs.

During the observations, I noted commonalities among all five Filipino immigrant families. I noticed that they were avid in displaying religious images, rosaries, Bibles, and Bible quotes on the walls. I also noticed that Filipino immigrant families were busy entertaining me. Because the participants knew I was a pastor, they were busy hosting me and making sure I was comfortable. While this response was not what I expected, it gave me insight into the personalities of Filipino immigrants as a hospitable people.

One of the families I observed consisted of an American husband married to a Filipino wife. During the visit, the wife was busy preparing dinner while their children were playing and running around. At the same time, the husband was watching a football game on the television and did not bother to help his wife nor care for the children, who were very loud. This is an example of the way Filipinos love to serve their families and are very patient in character.

In another situation, when I visited a family to conduct the participant observation, the family prepared a dinner and invited me to join them. The dinner table was full of Filipino dishes like adobo, pansit, sinigang, and rice. They also prepared a Filipino dessert called puto, which we all enjoyed. Before the dinner began, knowing that I am a pastor, the husband asked me to pray for the food. After praying, I noticed that the Filipino husband and wife did the sign of the cross, as is customary for Roman Catholics when they pray.

After the dinner, the husband invited me to their living room to watch an NBA game. While watching the game,

I noticed that the wife was the one cleaning the dining table and putting the dirty dishes into the dishwasher. I also noticed that one of their three children helped their mother in cleaning the kitchen. While watching the basketball game on television, the husband asked me about Philippine politics. Because the presidential election in the Philippines was coming up, he asked whom I would vote for in the coming election. Filipino immigrants who have dual citizenship are allowed to cast their votes through absentee voting. I responded that he could not vote because he was not able to go to Washington, DC, to register as an absentee voter. I noticed that the husband was very passionate about Philippine politics as he shared his many frustrations in the Philippines regarding different aspects like corruption, poverty, and criminality.

Such participant observations helped me to understand the Filipino immigrants' piety, family values, and interests. As religious people, Filipino immigrants highly value their Catholic faith. It is evident that Filipino immigrants are hospitable people. They also love to be visited and feel honored when a pastor visits them and prays for them. I also noticed that Filipino immigrants love to serve their families, particularly the Filipino women in the way they serve their American husbands. Filipino immigrants desire to talk about current events, especially the political situation of the Philippines.

── DATA COLLECTION AND MANAGEMENT ──

In addition to conducting interviews to gather the data needed for this research, I spent time observing individuals/families in their home environments. I asked to visit them and set up appointment times through face-to-face interaction, phone calls, and text messages. In this way, I was able to understand the lifestyles, values, and thought processes of participants, which helped me to collect relevant data for this study. As these are real people with privacy to protect, I will refer to them by their participant numbers.[74]

── INSTRUMENTATION ──

I used interviews and participant observations as instruments in collecting data. I followed Creswell and Poth's procedures in preparing and conducting interviews, as follows:

- Determine the research questions that will be answered by interviewees.
- Identify interviewees who can best answer these questions based on one of the purposeful sampling procedures.
- Distinguish the type of interview by determining what mode is practical and what interactions will net the most useful information to answer research questions.

- Collect data using adequate recording procedures when conducting one-on-one or focus group interviews.
- Design and use an interview protocol or interview guide.
- Refine the interview questions and the procedures through pilot testing.
- Locate a distraction-free place for conducting the interview.
- Obtain consent from the interviewee to participate in the study by completing a consent form approved by the human relations review board.
- As an interviewer, follow good interview procedures.
- Decide transcription logistics ahead of time.[75]

I also followed their protocols, as follows:
- Respect the site and disrupt as little as possible.
- Make sure that all participants receive the benefits.
- Avoid deceiving participants.
- Respect potential power imbalances.
- Avoid exploitation of participants.
- Avoid collecting harmful information.[76]

Thus, I was cautious not to disrupt the site and was mindful of the participants' privacy. I shared the outcome of the research to participants so they could also benefit from the study, which I described to them in detail before the interviews.[77] During the interviews, I respected the participants' answers to every question and was also careful not to use any data that might cause them harm. Participants were also given the opportunity to ask any questions regarding the research. However, to my surprise, no participants raised any questions about the study. At the end of the interview, I gave a small token of appreciation in the form of $25 Visa gift card to compensate their time and to offset any expenses incurred during the interviews.

DATA ANALYSIS

Sharing the results of these interviews required me to generate shared outcomes among the responses and discussions I enjoyed. These themes were based on my coding,[78] which began by identifying categories, themes, and codes, upon which I then expanded. Then I could offer detailed descriptions in the following chapters. The coding themes were gathered from every participants' perspective during the interview process.[79]

The table below lists the (five) themes and (thirty-two) subthemes that I used as analysis codes during manual coding. These became clear as they were repeated through the interview and analysis process.

THEME	SUBTHEME
Filipino immigrants' perceptions about Christianity	Catholicism viewed as Christianity in the Philippines Complexity of Christianity in the US Christianity and other religions compared Other Filipino immigrants' understanding of Christianity Filipino immigrants' questions about Christianity
Factors that contribute to the Filipino immigrants attending church	Socialization Influence from relatives Bible exposition Curiosity
Factors that inhibit the Filipino immigrants from attending church	Work schedule Feeling unaccepted Pandemic Tiredness Unsupportive people No children's ministry Parents do not go to church No hindrances
Church events that the Filipino immigrants want	Fellowships Visitations Inter-active worship service Community outreach Easter celebrations Thanksgiving celebrations Church retreats Children's activities
Needs of the Filipino immigrants that the church should help meet	Prayers Encouragement through social media Spiritual support Financial support Counseling Bible studies Church intervention

(Table 2)

I will discuss these in detail in the next three chapters.

CHAPTER 4:

TALKING ABOUT CHRISTIANITY

FILIPINO IMMIGRANTS' PERCEPTIONS ABOUT CHRISTIANITY

During the interviews, participants were asked the question, "In your understanding, how would you describe Christianity?" Each participant willingly answered the question. Sixteen of the participants had a specific answer, while one stated he had no comment.

Table 3 shows each Filipino immigrants' perception of Christianity.

— PERCEPTIONS ABOUT CHRISTIANITY —

PARTICIPANTS	IMMIGRANTS' PERCEPTIONS ABOUT CHRISTIANITY
Ruben	belief in Jesus Christ
Marie	good people
Edward	worshipping God
George	relationship
Randy	relationship
Albert	belief in Jesus
Donna	relationship
Tess	follow Jesus
Caleb	worshipping Jesus
Danny	follow the teachings of Jesus
Isabel	loving God
Robert	way of life
Alma	relationship with Jesus
Renato	belief in God that guides and protects
Lorna	believe in Jesus Christ
Rudy	imitators of Christ
Francis	no comment

(Table 3)

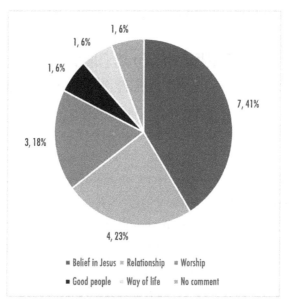

Immigrants' Perceptions of Christianity
(Chart 3)

As the chart shows, seven (41%) of the participants described Christianity as belief in Jesus Christ, and four (23%) believed that Christianity is about relationship. Clarifying questions indicated that their understanding of relationship can include relationship with God, relationship with other people, and family relationships. Moreover, three (18%) of the participants defined Christianity as worshipping God, worshipping Jesus, or going to church for repentance. The other three participants had answers that fall outside these general categories, with one (6%) looking at Christianity as good people, one (6%) stating that Christianity is a way of life, and one

(6%) saying he would not make any comment about it.

CATHOLICISM VIEWED AS CHRISTIANITY IN THE PHILIPPINES

To better understand how Filipino immigrants viewed Christianity before coming to the United States, each participant was asked, "What did you learn about Christianity while you were in the Philippines?" The majority of the participants were able to answer the question. However, two young adults indicated they did not have much understanding then because they were both very young when they left the country.

Most of the participants indicated that their perception was that it is all about Roman Catholicism. Lorna said, "Christianity in the Philippines was introduced by the Spaniards. So, a lot of local especially the older people, they just attached to being Catholic or Jesus Christ. Christianity was introduced so technically even if you don't like it, but because of the family around they will embrace Christianity."[80] Moreover, George and Francis believe that the majority of Filipinos in the Philippines are Catholics. Renato revealed that his understanding of Christianity emanates from his parents who were very active in their religious organization called Couples for Christ, a Roman Catholic activity. He added that he was also sent to De LaSalle, a Catholic school, where he was taught to be a good citizen and a good child of God. Alma stated that he attended a Catholic school and learned that there are many Christian communities and that one of the communities is the Roman Catholic. However, according to Alma, all Christian communities have the same common denominator, which is Jesus Christ.

Others shared a different understanding of Christianity while in the Philippines. Isabel responded, "Well, Christianity for us, in the Philippines, is more on a belief that there's a God that will protect you from when you were born until the day that you will die."[81] Isabel, who is a practicing Roman Catholic, mentioned that she and her family go to St. John Neumann for weekly mass. She added that Roman Catholicism is given importance in the Philippines because it is being included in every school's curriculum. In another response, Caleb focused on the activities of the Roman Catholic church. He grew up as a Catholic, and he understood the Trinity, mentioning God the Father, God the Son, and God the Holy Spirit. He added that Catholicism is Christianity. He also mentioned the devotion to saints and celebrating Fiestas, a religious festival in the Philippines in honor of a saint. P8 stated, "I went to a Catholic school, I was brought up in a Catholic church. So, everything that I learned about Christianity is based out of being Catholic."[82]

For Edward, Christianity revolves around three religious institutions. He said that Christianity in the Philippines is about Roman Catholics, Baptists, and the

Iglesia Ni Cristo, which is one of the biggest local religious groups in the Philippines. He added that Christianity in the Philippines is divided and is always in conflict with other religions. Edward added that the reason he said there were conflicts between religions was because of the regular debate among religious organizations which is televised nationwide.

Moreover, Robert believed that Catholicism has been in existence in the Philippines for many years. He said, "Christianity for me is a religion already coined in the Philippines."[83] He also claimed that Christianity can mean either being Catholic or being "born again." However, Donna stated that while living in the Philippines, he understood that Christianity is about having a relationship with God and that Christ lives within his heart.

COMPLEXITY OF CHRISTIANITY IN THE US

The interviews of seventeen participants revealed their perceptions of Christianity among Filipino immigrants while living in the United States. According to Marie and Tess, it was only when they migrated to the United States that they gained knowledge about the Bible and widened their understanding of Christianity. Alma was able to attend a Bible study for the first time after coming to the United States, although she stated that she has not been to any Christian church but only to a Roman Catholic church. Albert and Caleb stated that it was only when they migrated to the US that they learned there are different Protestant churches or denominations. Edward and George shared the same basic perception while living in the US. According to Edward, Christianity in the United States is more liberated as compared to the Philippines. He said that most Christians who come to church for Sunday services do not care about what they are wearing, they just come wearing shorts, T-shirts, and flip-flops. George said Christians in the United States are hard to identify, adding that you cannot tell someone is a Christian unless they tell you so.

A few participants indicated that living in the United States has given them a different perspective about Christianity. Randy stated that he understands that Christianity is about Christian values, responsibility, and obedience. Donna said she has learned the value of giving and having relationships with others. Francis said Christianity in the US is more about focusing on the Lord.

Robert declared that Christianity in the United States is about fellowshipping: "Christianity here is more of a fellowship and believing Jesus as Lord and Savior. It's basically fellowship. And every Sunday we attend a church. We do praise and worship. We do listen to the pastor for preaching, and then at the end, you can also ask for a prayer." Renato said that when he migrated to the United States, his faith was strengthened, and he learned how to pray for guidance.

Furthermore, Lorna said that US Christians has a shallow understanding of Christianity: "Christians in the US know about Christianity but do not practice what they know." Rudy said he learned nothing new about Christianity while living in the United States. He added that Christianity is about going to church every Sunday.

CHRISTIANITY AND OTHER RELIGIONS COMPARED

The third interview question asked of every participant was, "How does Christianity compare to other religions?" Three responded that other religions are idol worshippers. Specifically, the participants stated that they worship images, saints, and Mother Mary.

However, Donna and Caleb said that Christianity is about believing the Trinity, which is God the Father, God the Son, and God the Holy Spirit. Furthermore, they stated that Christianity believes in the Lordship of Jesus while other religions do not believe in Jesus. Alma stated, "I'm confused, to be honest, well, for Christianity compared to the other religion[s], like Muslim[s], they have different name for God, while Christianity believes in Jesus Christ."[84]

Five participants found similarities among the Gods of different religions. Edward believed that Christians and Muslims both worship the same God. Moreover,

Renato stated that although Christianity and other religions have different beliefs, they believe in the same God. George stated that "In Islam, they believe in Prophet Muhammad. In Catholicism, they put more emphasis on the saints and God, while Christian religion believes in God and the Holy Trinity. I think that's all the difference, but I think all of them view the same person. For Muslims it's Allah, which is also God and the same God for Catholics."[85] Moreover, Albert believed that there are similarities and differences between Christianity and other religions. A similarity is that both Christianity and other religions believe in God who is sovereign and created the universe. Regarding differences, Christians can have a personal relationship with God, while those of other religions, particularly Hinduism, believe God is far above them. The people do not have access to their God because that God is too high and mighty.

However, Rudy emphasized the similarities of religions based on the premise of becoming a good person. He stated that "there are some similarities to it, as far as I think, the premise or on the surface anyway. Because Christianity and other religion, we all preach about being a good person. So, in that regard, as far as being a good person, I think all religions are similar."[86]

Regarding Buddhism and Christianity, Tess believed that Buddhism is a way of life, whereas Christianity believes in the existence of God. She stated, "It's something that affects your whole life; it is something that affects your daily activities, your daily interactions with other people, and how you view things." Francis said that in Catholicism you can confess your sins to the priest, which contrasts with Protestantism, where people can directly confess to the Lord.

Danny claimed that Christianity is the only way to salvation and to God. In addition, he stated that he cannot compare Christianity with other religions because he lacks an understanding about the teachings of other religions. According to Isabel, Christianity is broader than other religions. However, she believes that there is no religion better than any other religion.

Robert and Lorna offered different perceptions of Christianity in comparison with other religions. For Robert, "Christianity is very lax, like, you literally can do whatever you want. And, like, other religions they are very strict in following their teachings." While Lorna understood Christianity as people who have a good heart, while people from other religions have an attitude or behavior that is not pleasing to others.

OTHER FILIPINO IMMIGRANTS' UNDERSTANDING OF CHRISTIANITY

The interview process involved asking participants about what they think other Filipino immigrants would say about Christianity. The data gathered show different perceptions of other Filipino immigrants based on the understanding of the participants. Four out of seventeen participants believed that other immigrants would not say anything against Christianity. Marie stated that when she had the chance to talk about Christianity with other Filipino immigrants, they immediately ended the conversation. Danny shared that other immigrants would not say anything against Christianity because they are Filipinos and Christianity is the dominant religion in the Philippines.

Isabel said that most immigrants are Catholics, and they will not say anything negative against other Christians. Moreover, she said that most Catholics believe that they are Christians and have the same belief as other Christians. Robert stated that other Filipino immigrants have a negative perception of Protestantism because they believe that Catholicism is the only true religion. However, Lorna stated that other Filipino immigrants believe that they are all Christians. Unfortunately, they will not engage in any conversation about Christianity because they migrated to the United States to work and not for religious reasons.

Other participants said they believe Filipino immigrants would say that Christianity is a way of life. George said they grew up as Catholics, and they are fine with it. However, Albert strongly stated that they are ignorant about Protestantism because they grew up as Roman Catholics and do not understand it. Another perception is that other

Filipino immigrants have high expectations for Christians, while Rudy said that other immigrants would think that Christianity is intimidating. Alma and Renato both said that Christianity is divided and has different practices.

When asked about what they think other Filipino immigrants would say about Christianity, Ruben said that he does not have any interactions with other immigrants. Randy thinks that other immigrants would just say to do good to get into heaven. Tess stated that other Filipino immigrants believe that Christianity is about praying to Mary and the saints. Caleb thought that other immigrants would say that Christianity is funny because they worship too loudly. Lastly, according to Rudy and Francis, Christianity is intimidating, and other Filipino immigrants do not want to be in a Christian environment.

FILIPINO IMMIGRANTS' QUESTIONS ABOUT CHRISTIANITY

I asked the seventeen participants about what questions they had regarding Christianity. Twelve participants responded and shared their thoughts about questions, and five participants said they had no questions.

Questions about Christianity

PARTICIPANTS	IMMIGRANTS' QUESTIONS ABOUT CHRISTIANITY
Ruben	No question
Marie	What is born again?
Edward	Is there life after death?
George	What is the difference between OT and NT?
Randy	When is second coming?
Albert	No question
Donna	How to understand the Bible?
Tess	No question
Caleb	How to get to heaven?
Danny	No question
Isabel	What is the difference between Christianity and other religions?
Robert	What is the scope of Christianity? What is religion?
Alma	No question
Renato	How strong am I as a believer?
Lorna	How to get to heaven?
Rudy	Am I doing enough?
Francis	Why do we evangelize?

(Table 4)

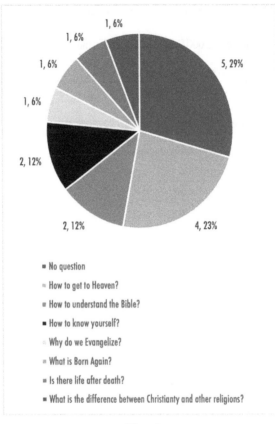

1, 6%

1, 6%

1, 6%

5, 29%

1, 6%

2, 12%

2, 12%

4, 23%

- No question
- How to get to Heaven?
- How to understand the Bible?
- How to know yourself?
- Why do we Evangelize?
- What is Born Again?
- Is there life after death?
- What is the difference between Christianty and other religions?

(Chart 4)

Four (23%) of the participants asked a question about how to get to heaven. Caleb stated that the biggest question that he had in life growing up as a Catholic was how to get to heaven. He added that all he knows is for him to be a good person. He also believes that if he does good, then God would reward him and allow him to enter heaven. Lorna stated that although her question was about how to get to heaven, he believed that the question will be answered later when he gets to heaven.

Two (12%) of the participants asked about how to understand the Bible. Donna stated that when she asked someone to explain the Bible, they always found it hard. George's question was, "What should we follow, the Old Testament or New Testament teachings?"[87]

Two (12%) participants had a question related to understanding their inner being. Renato stated, "For me, I think the question that comes in my mind is how strong I am as a believer and how strongly I am to understand about my concern as a Christian."[88] Rudy simply asked, "Am I doing enough?"

Four of the answers to the question can be put in separate categories. One (6%) participant, Francis, asked why we evangelize, whereas Marie (6%) asked a question about being born again. She added that the term "born again" sounds ridiculous. She asked how that would happen and how, after you were born as a baby and grew up, could you be born again. She said the term is confusing and should be explained. One (6%) of the participants, Edward, stated that the question he had in mind about Christianity was about life after death. He would like to know what will happen to those people who died and have never found out about Christianity. Isabel would like to know what the difference between Christianity and other religions, such as Scientology.

FILIPINO IMMIGRANTS' PERCEPTIONS ABOUT CHRISTIANITY

The data collected clearly indicate that the immigrants' perception of Christianity centers on Catholicism. They believe that Catholicism and Christianity are the same religion that teaches believers to obey God's commandments. Catholicism was handed down to them from their parents who were also devout Roman Catholics. One of the participants stated that Catholicism runs through the family. Furthermore, their belief in Catholicism was also heavily influenced by schools where Catholic teachings are part of the school's curriculum.

As Catholics, they were taught to pray the rosary as their way of connecting to God. They were also taught to pray to the saints for guidance and protection. Furthermore, Catholics have several religious practices, and one of those is what they called "fiestas," a celebration in honor of a saint. This is the time when Roman Catholics come together for special services, processions, and celebrations. Although some participants admitted they did not have enough understanding of the Bible, they believed as Catholics that God lives within their hearts and that doing good to other people is what they need to do to become better people.

The research also indicated that Filipino migration to the United States has made them change their perception of Christianity. Coming to the US opened their understanding that other religions exist besides Catholicism. One of the participants stated that migrating made him aware of the existence of Protestant churches. The participants said that being away from their families in the Philippines and living in the United States, either alone or with their families, enabled them to begin to realize the importance of having a relationship with Jesus, reading their Bibles, and socializing with other Filipino immigrants.

My findings further show that the Filipino immigrants were more open to the gospel while in the US. The immigrants were willing to accept changes, including an understanding of Christianity. I note that this supports the claim of Mina Roces that "the very act of migration, of relocating to a new culture and society, introduces new possibilities and, by extension, potential for fundamental change. Freed from the rules of established cultural practice and the surveillance of family, kin, and society, the migrant discovers that it is now possible to reinvent oneself."[89]

There is general agreement from all three age groups that Christianity and Catholicism are essentially synonymous. Three quarters of the young adults, two-thirds of those middle-aged, and half of the elderly participants identified Christianity with Catholicism.

CHAPTER 5

GOING TO CHURCH

FACTORS THAT CONTRIBUTE TO FILIPINO IMMIGRANTS ATTENDING CHURCH

The participants were asked, "In your experience, what has drawn you to attend a church gathering?" and, "Have people you know who attend a church been a factor in your decision to attend church gatherings? If so, in what ways?" All seventeen responded.

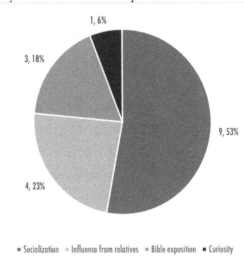

What Draws Immigrants to Attend Church

(Chart 5)

SOCIALIZATION

Nine (53%) participants indicated that socialization is what draws them to attend a church gathering. For George, he added that as an immigrant who does not know any Filipinos in the area, going to the Catholic church would help him socialize with other Filipinos. Donna stated that she noticed that the people in the church are happy and peaceful people. Tess said that when she attended a church gathering, she felt the love and being welcomed in the church. Lorna said that it was because of emptiness that she decided to attend church gatherings. Marie and George stated that what draws them to attend a church gathering is meeting new friends and connecting with other immigrants.

Four (23%) of the participants stated that what draws them is the influence of their relatives. Randy stated that he attends a church because his parents attend the church. Albert and Isabel said that it is because of their family that they, too, attend the church, while Francis stated that it was through his wife that he was influenced to attend a church.

Three (18%) participants said what draws immigrants to attend church is Bible exposition. Caleb said he wanted to hear a pastor explaining the Bible because in the Catholic church, the priest does not explain it well. Isabel stated that she wanted to learn from the teachings of Jesus, while Alma stated that she wanted her faith to be strengthened.

According to Ruben, curiosity is another factor that

encourages people to go to church. He said, he was curious to know about Catholicism, their beliefs, and practices.

DISCUSSING FACTORS THAT CONTRIBUTE TO FILIPINO IMMIGRANTS ATTENDING CHURCH

I asked the participants, "In your experience, what has drawn you to attend a church gathering?" Nine (53%) said that socialization was the major contributing factor that would make them attend church. This factor supports the literature review stating that immigrants are those people who move out of their home country to settle down in a new country.

It's important to remember that being an immigrant involves some emotional distress and loneliness in moving away from the familiar to the unknown. Being away from loved ones in the Philippines would be the hardest thing that an immigrant would experience. As Renato said, "The reason I am attending church gatherings is that I live in the United States alone. I do not have any family members with me, so I need to mingle with other people." George, being a new immigrant who did not know any Filipinos in the area, said that going to Catholic church would help him socialize with other Filipinos. Marie and George also said they attended church to meet new friends and to connect with other immigrants.

Another factor that encourages immigrants to attend church is the influence of relatives. Four (23%) participants indicated they have been influenced by their relatives to attend church. Filipinos are known to be family oriented. Born and raised in the Philippines, I have personal experience with how Filipinos put their families before anything else. Edward admitted that the reason he does not go to church is that his parents do not go. Two other participants, Ruben, and Francis, claimed that the reason they attend church is because of the influence of their relatives. For Ruben, he only attends church because his parents are going to church, while Francis said that he goes to church because his wife insisted that he should go with her to the church.

Bible exposition is another factor. Three (18%) of the participants claimed that proper explanation of the Bible has made them attend church. However, one participant (6%), Rudy, stated that it was curiosity that drew him to church. He said he was curious to know about Catholics, their beliefs and practices, probably because when he was growing up he was taught some about Catholicism and moving to the US has given him access to other religious faiths.

FACTORS THAT INHIBIT FILIPINO IMMIGRANTS FROM ATTENDING CHURCH

Meanwhile, an important aspect in developing an effective evangelism strategy for Filipino immigrants is to understand why they do not go to church. I asked the participants, "In your experience, what has kept you from attending church gatherings?" and, "Have people you know who attend a church been a factor in your decision not to attend church gatherings? If so, in what ways?" Analysis of the data gathered led me to the discovery of factors affecting the immigrants from attending church gatherings.

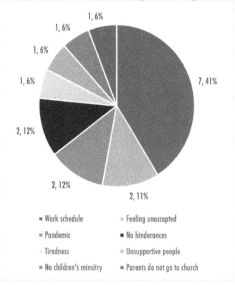

What Inhibits Immigrants from Attending Church

(Chart 6)

The major factor that inhibits Filipino immigrants from attending church concerns work schedules. Seven (41%) of the seventeen participants were limited in their ability to attend church because they work on Sundays. Tess said she often needs to work on Sundays. Alma also stated that her work schedule has kept her from attending church gatherings, and Renato clarified that, as a nurse, he needs to work even on Sundays. "When asked during the interview about what kept him from attending church, he simply said, "Oh! My heart says I have to go to church, but right now, with my situation, I have to work week-end[s], and I have to work Saturdays and Sundays."

Here, it is important to note that the major reason for migration is economic disparity. Filipino immigrants are working to send money back to the Philippines. The immigrants' desire to help their families financially has made them neglect the importance of weekly church gatherings for their spiritual needs. Without debate, the primary reason for migration was to improve the immigrants' living conditions, often accomplished by working long hours. However, the data show that working also affects the immigrants' ability to care for their spiritual needs. P4 stated that her work schedule has kept her from attending church gatherings.

It's unsurprising, then, that work schedules would be major factors for the working-aged interviewees (eighteen to thirty years old) and middle-aged (thirty-one to fifty). The older participants (fifty years and older) did not consider work hours as a factor in their absence from church. An older participant, Ruben, claimed there was nothing stopping him from going to church. The elderly participants in this study were all retired from their jobs.

For another factor, two (12%) participants said that feeling unaccepted has kept them from attending church. Francis had an experience in the church when he was ignored, and no one came to him when he asked for help. Lorna stated that what has kept her from attending is that the church has not been welcoming. This factor should sound an alarm for the church. The analysis of the data indicates that there is something that the church is missing. The church is supposed to be a place of love and acceptance.

Another factor was the pandemic. Two (12%) said gathering in large groups is unwise. Both George and Donna stated that COVID-19 has kept them from going to church. Neither participant elaborated as to how COVID-19 has affected their attending church gatherings.

Being tired was a minor factor that inhibits Filipino immigrants from church attendance, according to Albert (6%), although he did not elaborate on what makes him feel tired.

Another factor was that people in the church are seen as unsupportive. Robert (6%) indicated that seeing people who are unsupportive discouraged him from participating in any church gatherings. According to Robert, "If the people themselves do not support each other, like brotherly support, then I would just keep myself at home and learn the doctrine by myself."

A family with little children tends to go to a church that takes care of their little ones during services. In this research, Caleb (6%) indicated that a church without children's ministry would not attract him. Caleb, who has three little children, stated that he needs someone to take care of his children in church so he can focus on worship services. Similarly, Edward (6%) said what kept him from attending church is that his parents do not go to church. Clearly, family is a significant issue.

I also asked participants if there were people who have been a factor in their decision not to attend church. Twelve participants stated that there was no specific person or group of people who attended a church who were a factor in their decision not to attend, but three said that some people were a factor. They cited the pride of those people and also for personal reasons. During the interview, one of the participants, Robert, made it clear that the reason he sometimes does not go to church is because of the people in the church who were unappreciative. He said, "When you come to church, and you're not appreciated, and you have differences in your opinions and differences in the way you view things as a whole, it makes you not attend anymore. That will discourage me because there is really nothing that we can agree on."

In addition, two participants stated that not knowing

anyone from the church and meeting people in the church who were not appreciative has kept them from attending.

Finally, two (11%) participants said that there is nothing that restricts them from attending church. Ruben stated that he had no comment, and Randy clarified that there is nothing that hinders him from going to church, which indicates there is also nothing to motivate him to go.

CHAPTER 6:
NEEDS OF FILIPINO IMMIGRANTS THE CHURCH SHOULD HELP MEET

The interviews greatly concerned what immigrant needs the church should help meet. According to the participants, meeting these needs would help them in their daily lives.

As I discussed above, the literature supports this claim that evangelism should be practical and adaptable. Most Christians today understand that evangelism is sharing the faith with someone else; however, as I said, evangelism needs to be practical. The practical approach to evangelism includes addressing the needs of the people.

The Bible tells believers not only to love with words but also through action (1 John 3:18). This reminds all Christians and churches to practically live out their faith. Christians are commanded to love and help those who are in need. Another passage of Scripture that reminds Christians about meeting the needs of others is in James 2:16, "If one of you says to them 'Go in peace; keep warm and well fed,' but does nothing about their physical needs, what good is it?"

Unsurprisingly, the most general way to describe

Filipino immigrants' needs is "support." As an immigrant myself, I have experienced difficulties in adjusting to the new culture. I remember in 2007, when my three-year-old son and I were in Manila International Airport waiting to get on board for our first international flight to join my wife in the United States who came two months ahead of us. It was a long flight that we needed to endure. Our first stop was Hong Kong, and then we got on board for our next flight to Chicago. Finally, I said to myself, *The American dream*. The fifteen-hour flight ended at Chicago O'Hare International Airport, it was winter, and almost all domestic flights were cancelled. The first thing that came to my mind was to call my wife to let her know about the cancellation of our flight to Columbia. However, my cellphone battery died, and I realized that my charger was in my checked luggage. I looked around to see who could help us—and thank God there were two officers at the counter. Armed with very little English and thick Filipino accent, I tried to communicate, but with very few sentences to communicate, it put me into an embarrassing and unforgettable moment. The exact words I said to the officers were, "Can I get your phone to call my wife?" I heard one of the officers say, "This guy is stupid." My first two hours in a foreign land as an immigrant made me stupid.

One of the many struggles that I went through was communication, and although not all immigrants have issues with communication, many find it hard to communicate well in English. As a Filipino immigrant, my home country was blessed with 180 dialects, where two of the dialects I can fluently speak and write. English would be my third. I hate going to the fast-food drive-thru because of the fear of miscommunication. I would rather go inside and point my finger to get a cheeseburger and French fries. Another thing is when we do grocery shopping, I hate going to the counter thinking that the cashier might ask me a question or start a conversation. What would I say? I would always tell my wife to go ahead and pay, and then I would wait for her outside.

I remember in 2010, I was a new student here at CIU. On the first day of class, our professor asked everyone in the class to introduce themselves. When it was my turn, I was proud to tell everyone that my name is Jake Bolotano, and I was born and raised in the Philippines. When I sat down, my classmate sitting next to me told me that I have a nice name. They said, "What is your real name?"

Sadiri Joy Tira and Enoch Wan claimed that the factors affecting the movement of people are the following: "war, natural disasters . . . the breaking up of states . . . demographic changes in aging nations . . . urbanization, personal development, educational advance, diplomatic and military assignments, and economic disparities between developing and developed countries coupled with an increasingly mobile labour force" (Tira and Wan 2021, 1).

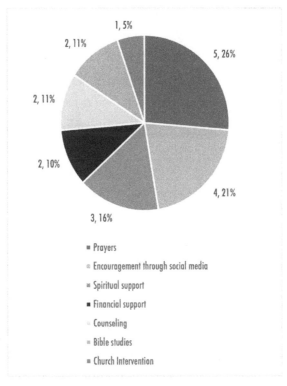

1, 5%

2, 11%

5, 26%

2, 11%

2, 10%

4, 21%

3, 16%

- Prayers
- Encouragement through social media
- Spiritual support
- Financial support
- Counseling
- Bible studies
- Church Intervention

**Immigrants' Needs That the
Church Should Help Meet**

(Chart 7)

PRAYERS

Chart 7 shows that five (26%) of the participants stated that they need prayers. According to them, prayer would help them with their daily lives. During the participant observations, I noticed that the immigrants would love to be visited and prayed for. Marie stated during the interviews that she needs prayer, she believes in prayers, and that it can move mountains.

Of these five participants, three were middle-aged, and two were young adults. Interestingly, none of the older participants indicated their daily lives require prayer.

More generally speaking, three (16%) of the participants said they need spiritual advice or spiritual support. Alma stated that as a new immigrant, he needs someone to guide him spiritually. Moreover, Edward stated that, as a young man, he needs spiritual guidance to grow and become mature in faith. This finding shows that Filipino immigrants desire to be with someone who can spiritually guide them in their daily lives. The immigrants' desire to have someone to guide them spiritually should make the church more actively involved in discipleship. This research finding is an opportunity for the church to develop or make an assessment about their evangelism and discipleship programs, as I will discuss in the final chapter.

Another type of support is financial. Two (11%) participants indicated that financial assistance is needed to help other immigrants as they transition in their new culture. Randy clarified that when an immigrant experiences financial need, it would be nice for the church to reach out and extend help. He added that he personally experienced help when his son was hospitalized. The church gathered and pooled their resources to help him. It was an unfortunate moment in the life of Randy and the entire family, when their youngest son, Emmanuel, was diagnosed with cardiomyopathy, a disease of the heart muscle that makes it harder for the heart to pump blood to the rest of the body. Upon learning the needs of the family, the church immediately organized a team to lead a fundraising campaign to help the family with their expenses.

Emotional support became the focus when two (11%) of the Filipino immigrants discussed needing counseling. Donna said that people always have problems, and through counseling they will be able to find comfort and refuge.

As for educational support, there is no doubt that Bible studies help every individual in their spiritual growth, although only two (11%) participants shared this specifically as a need. Robert saw the importance of Bible studies in his life. He stated that he needs to join Bible studies to grow and become mature. P6 stated that he needs to be in a Bible study group where he can talk to other people on a smaller scale rather than as a member of a congregation during service.

Another means of discussing support is direct intervention on the part of the church to help immigrants in their lives. According to Ruben, the church should intervene in helping to resolve immigrants' problems. He added that the church should get involved in helping those families dealing with different issues in life.

Considering the state of today's culture, Filipino or

not, it's to be expected that much of this support would be appreciated when delivered through social media. Four (21%) of the participants saw social media as an important tool in their daily lives, a number that can only grow over time. Tess said she wants to have something to listen to from the church via a social media platform such as YouTube, Facebook, or podcasting. For Isabel, since she worked on weekends, she stated that she would love for a church to have the sermon uploaded online so she could watch it anytime and grow spiritually. Alma stated that people today are into social media, adding that the church should use social media as an avenue to reach out to immigrants by posting encouraging words or Bible verses. She further stated that doing so will help immigrants in their spiritual condition. Lorna encouraged the church to use social media to invite immigrants by sending them messages through text and email. Again, social media outreach would be a good way to make the activities of the church part of Filipino immigrants' daily lives.

CHURCH EVENTS THAT THE FILIPINO IMMIGRANTS WANT

After hearing about needs, I had to ask what the church could do not just to support those needs, but "to make it more inviting for you to attend." The participants had many varied answers.

Church Events That Filipino Immigrants Want

PARTICIPANTS	CHURCH EVENTS
Ruben	Visitation, Picnics
Marie	Easter celebration
Edward	Church retreat, Interactive sermon
George	Easter celebration
Randy	Lunch after service
Albert	Meeting new immigrants
Donna	Serve in Harvest Hope Food Bank
Tess	Community outreach
Caleb	Childcare program, Worship band
Danny	Good sermon
Isabel	Fellowships
Robert	Visitation, Small group gatherings
Alma	Social gatherings, thanksgiving
Renato	Building relationships
Lorna	Thanksgiving, fellowships
Rudy	Reaching out to other immigrants
Francis	Social gatherings, Good church environment

(Table 5)

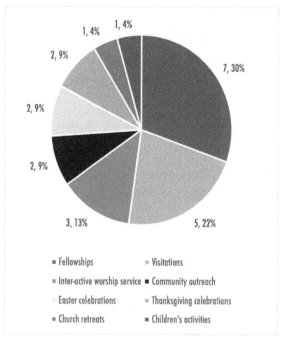

Pie chart labels:

1, 4%   1, 4%
1, 4%
2, 9%
7, 30%
2, 9%
2, 9%
3, 13%   5, 22%

Legend:
■ Fellowships   ▨ Visitations
▨ Inter-active worship service ■ Community outreach
▨ Easter celebrations   ▨ Thanksgiving celebrations
■ Church retreats   ■ Children's activities

(Chart 8)

All seventeen participants said there are events that they want for their church. My analysis of the data gathered revealed that fellowship is the most important event for immigrants. Seven (30%) of the participants specifically said they want to attend church for fellowship. Although fellowship comes in many forms, the immigrants understood fellowships as picnics, having lunch after service, small group gathering for whatever purpose, and Bible studies. In my interview with the participants, Alma reiterated that having fellowship would help the church to build relationships with immigrants.

Fellowship appears to be more important to the middle-aged and elderly participants than it is for the young adults. Of the seven participants who indicated the importance of fellowship, only one was from the young adult group.

Fellowship also comes from visitation. Five (22%) participants discussed the value of having someone from the church visit them. Ruben suggested that the church should create a team to visit immigrants and invite them to the church. One of the mistakes that most churches are making today is that they are just waiting for people to come to church. Another participant (Rudy) in this study suggested the church should be visiting the immigrants in their houses even if it is uncomfortable for the church to do so. Although it will be challenging, the church should be more creative in making ways to connect with immigrants.

Interviewees also touched on the desire for an interactive worship service. Three (13%) participants wanted this event for the church. Edward noted that he wants an engaging worship service. However, George stated that an engaging church should have a good worship band. He added that he loves a church that has good audio with a projector for PowerPoint presentations. As a strategy to invite immigrants to come to worship, the Filipino American Friendship Ministry of Christ should invest in the said equipment.

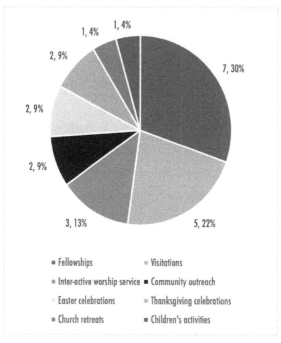

1, 4% 1, 4%

1, 4%

2, 9%

7, 30%

2, 9%

2, 9%

3, 13%   5, 22%

■ Fellowships   ▨ Visitations
▨ Inter-active worship service ■ Community outreach
▨ Easter celebrations   ▨ Thanksgiving celebrations
■ Church retreats   ■ Children's activities

(Chart 8)

All seventeen participants said there are events that they want for their church. My analysis of the data gathered revealed that fellowship is the most important event for immigrants. Seven (30%) of the participants specifically said they want to attend church for fellowship. Although fellowship comes in many forms, the immigrants understood fellowships as picnics, having lunch after service, small group gathering for whatever purpose, and Bible studies. In my interview with the participants, Alma reiterated that having fellowship would help the church to build relationships with immigrants.

Fellowship appears to be more important to the middle-aged and elderly participants than it is for the young adults. Of the seven participants who indicated the importance of fellowship, only one was from the young adult group.

Fellowship also comes from visitation. Five (22%) participants discussed the value of having someone from the church visit them. Ruben suggested that the church should create a team to visit immigrants and invite them to the church. One of the mistakes that most churches are making today is that they are just waiting for people to come to church. Another participant (Rudy) in this study suggested the church should be visiting the immigrants in their houses even if it is uncomfortable for the church to do so. Although it will be challenging, the church should be more creative in making ways to connect with immigrants.

Interviewees also touched on the desire for an interactive worship service. Three (13%) participants wanted this event for the church. Edward noted that he wants an engaging worship service. However, George stated that an engaging church should have a good worship band. He added that he loves a church that has good audio with a projector for PowerPoint presentations. As a strategy to invite immigrants to come to worship, the Filipino American Friendship Ministry of Christ should invest in the said equipment.

Community outreach is another event and means of fellowship that came up during the interview process. Two (9%) of the participants indicated they have an interest in community outreach. The participants noted that serving in Harvest Hope Food Bank would be a good ministry. Lorna stated that she was invited by a friend to serve at the Harvest Hope Food Bank, where she found out that there were many homeless people waiting in line to receive a bag of food. She added that such a ministry could positively impact the church's evangelism efforts. Moreover, community outreaches are a good venue to introduce the church to the community.

As part of that, Easter and Thanksgiving celebrations are the annual events that the Filipino immigrants want to participate in. Two (9%) participants indicated their interest in each of these events. However, George (4%) shows interest in church retreats, while Isabel (4%) showed interest in children's activities.

———— PRACTICAL IMPLICATIONS ————

At this point, after having given voice to the lived experiences of the Filipino immigrants who agreed to speak to me, it's time to turn to specific and practical activities the church can undergo to reach out to the Filipino immigrant community in Columbia, South Carolina.

Although there is plenty of literature that supports

evangelism, discipleship, and missions, there is no specific literature about a strategy to evangelize Filipino immigrants. This research has brought to light what Columbia's Filipino church can do to develop an effective evangelism strategy for Filipino immigrants. The seventeen Filipino immigrants who participated in this study shared their concepts of Christianity, what drew them to attend church, what would inhibit them from attending, and the programs and activities that they wanted for the church. The analysis of the data gathered through interviews and participant observations has led to my development of the following evangelism strategy for Filipino immigrants.

FELLOWSHIPS

Seven (30%) of the participants wanted the church to have opportunities to fellowship. Although fellowship comes in many forms, Ruben stated that he would like the church to have picnics and invite other immigrants who do not go to church. For Randy, it is important to have fellowship or lunch after the service. He added that he finds it interesting to socialize after the service. Isabel said that fellowshipping would help every member strengthen relationships with immigrants. Alma stated that fellowship events can help the church invite more immigrants to come and will make them feel comfortable. However, Lorna felt that visiting Filipino immigrants in their houses and having small gatherings there for fellowship would encourage them to attend church gatherings. Furthermore, Robert and Francis also indicated the importance of fellowshipping. According to Francis, weekly fellowship would help build relationship with other immigrants.

Fellowship seems important for Filipino immigrants because it helps them socialize with other immigrants. As stated in the preceding sections, Filipino immigrants feel lonely, particularly those who are new and those who do not have their families with them. The data revealed that Filipino immigrants would love to socialize with other immigrants.

To respond to this need, I am going to challenge The Filipino American Friendship Ministry of Christ church to organize fellowship events like picnics, Bible study groups, and karaoke events for Filipinos to socialize and make them feel comfortable in church settings. These events will enable the church to reach out to immigrants more effectively with the message of Christ.

Other events that the church can organize for Filipino immigrants include sports activities like basketball or volleyball. These sports are common in the Philippines, and Filipinos love to play them. Furthermore, the church will plan to have mid-week church activities for those who are not able to attend church due to work.

VISITATIONS

Ruben said that the church should create a program where a team can visit immigrants in their homes and invite them to church. He said a church should create a program to visit new immigrants and help them in their transition to their new culture. He added that as an immigrant, he looks for a community that would help him in many aspects of being a new immigrant. Others reiterated the importance of visitation. Robert stated that a church should have a program where they can continue to reach out to Filipino immigrants. In addition, Alma emphasized that a church should go out to build relationships with the immigrants. Renato claimed that the church should visit immigrants even if it is uncomfortable for the church to do so. Renato understood that most church members and leaders have their own family to attend to and jobs that keep them busy. However, he felt that a visit from the church would encourage him and his family.

One of the important aspects of the ministry of the church is visitation to those who are not part of the church. As indicated in the interview process, Filipino immigrants do not go to church because they do not know anyone from the church. To visit someone indicates that the one being visited is valued. During participant observations, I noticed that immigrants are excited to have other people visit. Moreover, visiting immigrants in their homes would make them feel special and highly regarded.

As a response to this finding, the Filipino American Friendship Ministry of Christ will create a visiting team of two to four people. This team will be composed of a married couple who are mature Christians and actively involved in the church. The team will identify the immigrants and will make an appointment for visitation. During the visit, the team will introduce themselves and the church. They may also bring a small token such as cookies or donuts together with the church pamphlets and other related information to be given to the immigrants. This ministry should encourage the immigrants to trust the sincerity of the church in welcoming them into the community.

INTERACTIVE WORSHIP SERVICE

Three participants stated that the church should have an interactive worship service. For Edward, a church would be more inviting if there is an interactive sermon because he would feel he was being included in the service. Additionally, Caleb clarified that he would love to participate in a church where there are good worship services with a good worship team. Francis stated that he wanted to see a church where there are good relationships between members and a good church environment.

Worship services should be engaging and participatory. Some of the current church attendees are nurses who work at night. They indicated that they cannot attend church because they need to sleep. Therefore, as the pastor of the church, I will recommend to the leadership that other services should be organized during weekdays. I will also recommend the purchase of additional musical instruments and upgrading the equipment to make it more interactive. These changes in the church will lead to more Filipino immigrants attending church services.

COMMUNITY OUTREACH

Donna and Tess (9%) indicated that they wanted church to have a community outreach program. Tess said, "I've done some volunteer work at the Harvest Hope Food Bank. It would be nice to have a program like that community outreach."

Reaching out to the community is the church's response to Jesus' sermon on the mount, in which he said Christians should be salt and light to the community (Matt. 5:13-16). It is also a way for the church to be introduced to the community. The research study shows that Filipino immigrants want to join a church that is involved in community outreach.

In this regard, I will make a recommendation to the church leadership to identify community outreaches and invite Filipino immigrants to participate. Such ministry should encourage growth in the church as it mobilizes immigrants in serving the community.

CELEBRATIONS

Marie and George (9%) said they love to attend Easter celebrations such as Easter egg hunts where their children can participate. They added that it is also a good venue to invite other immigrants to participate in church services. I will take advantage of the Easter celebration to gather the immigrants with their families and children. The church will set a time at the park on Easter Sunday to celebrate and have their children enjoy an Easter egg hunt. This event will be followed by a picnic to engage other immigrants and build relationships.

Meanwhile, Alma and Lorna (9%) said they would attend a church to celebrate Thanksgiving. They added that there will always be Filipino parties during the Thanksgiving celebrations. Although we do not celebrate Thanksgiving in the Philippines, this is the celebration that we embrace since we migrated to the United States. Moreover, they taught that the church could use it to build relationships among Filipino immigrants. This celebration is an opportunity for the church to invite immigrants in the area for a meal. This can also be a time when immigrants feel relaxed and comfortable. In this setting, the church can also talk about the gospel and invite immigrants to come to church.

CHILDREN'S ACTIVITIES

Children can be involved at times that are not formal celebrations. I will recommend to the Filipino American Friendship Ministry of Christ church that they organize a team of volunteers to take care of the children according to age groups. During "children's time," the church will organize group games and will also provide materials like coloring books, children's toys, and light snacks as needed.

CHURCH RETREATS

In addition to celebration, and to involve adults, the church may organize retreats. Edward (6%) said he wants a church to have retreats where they can spend time with other immigrants away from home. The literature also indicates that participants want a church that sets aside time periodically for retreats, when members spend a few days together away from the church for spiritual purposes. This is also a time when immigrants can have a few days off from work to enjoy their time with friends and families. The church should plan regarding venues, topics, and the people to invite.

PRAYERS

I explained that I personally was asked to join in prayer at a Filipino home, indicating immigrants have high regard for prayers. I recommend that the church not hesitate to ask immigrants about how the church can pray for them and that the church should organize a prayer ministry. This ministry will be responsible for collecting prayer requests and conducting weekly prayer meetings.

SPIRITUAL SUPPORT

To address immigrants' spiritual needs, church members should make themselves available to comfort them when they are going through difficult times, pray, encourage, and give spiritual advice when needed. The church should also be available to celebrate with immigrants in their joyous moments.

To provide spiritual support, pastors, church leaders, and members should help immigrants when they are grieving the death of a loved one. The church should help and coordinate with the family about any arrangements for funerals and church services. Furthermore, the church can also provide guidance and prayers for those who are making important decisions, such as buying a home, finding a job, or moving to another location. In addition, the church can provide spiritual support to immigrants by giving them Christian reading materials.

FINANCIAL SUPPORT

It's vital to bear in mind that it often takes time for immigrants to find jobs. The church, being the hands and feet of Jesus, should take this opportunity to reach out with financial help. I will recommend that the church allocate an amount to assist immigrants in their times of need. Although the Filipino church is a small community church and does not have a large budget, the church can create a fund intended for the immediate needs of the immigrants. This action by the church should help immigrants to see the love of Christ through the church.

COUNSELING

Counseling is another resource the church should offer to immigrants. Living in a new culture entails psychological, emotional, and mental issues. One of the participants stated that he has been in the US for a year and a half and did not know anyone in the community. He said that living by himself made him lonely. He also mentioned that since he does not have a car, he just stays in his apartment and calls an Uber driver to take him to work. I, as an immigrant pastor, went through the same emotional and psychological problems as a new immigrant. Counseling should be an effective evangelism strategy for Filipino immigrants in Columbia. The church through its membership will identify professional counselors who are willing to lead the ministry. Other option would be hiring a professional counselor. This will certainly help the church in addressing immigrants' emotional, mental, psychological, and spiritual needs.

BIBLE STUDIES

A correct interpretation of the gospel will help immigrants to understand that Christianity and Catholicism are not the same. It is the responsibility of every Christian to proclaim the gospel in its intended meaning to avoid misleading those who will listen. During the interviews, a participant stated that he wanted a pastor to explain the Bible because the priest in the Catholic church did not explain it well.

To help immigrants grow in their knowledge of the Bible, the church will need to identify immigrants and invite them to join existing Bible study groups. Currently, the church has Wednesday Bible study for family, Saturday women's fellowship, and Saturday men's Bible study group. However, if immigrants feel uncomfortable joining the existing Bible study groups, the elders may visit the immigrants in their houses and have Bible studies with them. This approach should be effective because immigrants can freely share their thoughts about the Bible and ask questions without feeling intimidated.

CHURCH INTERVENTION

My research showed me that participants need the church to intervene in resolving conflict among the immigrants. While it is unavoidable that misunderstandings may occur, the church can help facilitate conflict resolution. In this regard, I will recommend that the pastor of the church, along with the elders, will handle problems of conflict resolution. This ministry can also greatly impact the conflicting parties as well as the Filipino community.

These practical implications of the research findings will help me, as a pastor, to effectively share the gospel with Filipino immigrants. It will also help the Filipino American Friendship Ministry of Christ church to grow in her weekly attendance and membership. Another practical implication that this research will bring to other Filipino churches, church leaders, and all Christians is that it will serve them as a guide to effectively share the gospel with Filipino immigrants.

ENCOURAGEMENT THROUGH SOCIAL MEDIA

And again, I urge the church to use social media because immigrants are busy working and do not have enough time to attend church services. Social media allow organizations to stay connected. I recommend that the church Sunday services be broadcast live through its Facebook page. The church will also post a weekly Bible passage and upload devotional videos to encourage those who are not able to attend church and stay connected. The church will also set up a website where immigrants can find important information about the church's ministries. Regular updates and uploading of photos will be conducted through the church's social media accounts.

READING LIST

Addison, Steve. *Movements That Change the World: Five Keys to Spreading the Gospel*. Rev. ed. Downers Grove, Ill: IVP Books, 2011.

Agee, Jane. "Developing Qualitative Research Questions: A Reflective Process." *International Journal of Qualitative Studies in Education* 22, no. 4 (2009): 431–47. https://doi.org/10.1080/09518390902736512

Aleinik, Volha. "Evangelism as Authentic Discipleship." *International Review of Mission* 103, no. 1 (2014): 116–20. http://doi.org/10.1111/irom.12048

Arthur, Eddie. "Missio Dei and the Mission of the Church." Wycliffe Global Alliance. https://www.wycliffe.net/more-about-what-we-do/papers-and-articles/missio-dei-and-the-mission-of-the-church

Badshah, Nadeem. "Thou Shall Not Commit Social Media Offenses: Faith Groups Back Church of England's Digital Charter." *Eastern Eye*, July 19, 2019.

Barnett, Mike, and Robin Martin. 2012. *Discovering the Mission of God: Best Missional Practices for the 21st Century*. Downers Grove, IL: IVP Academic.

Bosscher, Emily S. "Meet Generation Z: Understanding and Reaching the New Post-Christian World." *Christian Scholar's Review*, no. 2: 201.

Bourna, Jeremy. "What Is Evangelism?" Zondervan Academic.
https://zondervanacademic.com/blog/evangelism

Burger, John. "Filipinos Prepare for 500th Anniversary
of Receiving Christianity. Reflect on Their Role
in Evangelization." Aleteia, January 31, 2019.
https://aleteia.org/2019/01/28/filipinos-pre-
pare-for-500th-anniversary-of-receiving-christiani-
ty-but-also-reflect-on-their-role-in-evangelization

Carey, George. "Preaching Christ in a Broken World." *The
Mission of an Evangelist: Amsterdam 2000; A Conference
of Preaching Evangelists*. Minneapolis, MN: Worldwide
Publishers, 2001.

Carr, Caleb T., and Rebecca Hayes. "Social Media: Defining,
Developing, and Divining." *Atlantic Journal of
Communication* 23, no. 1 (2015):46–65.
https://doi.org/http://doi.org/
10.1080/15456870.2015.972282

Carson, Donald A. "Do the Work of an
Evangelist." *Themelios* 39, no. 1 (2014): 1–4.

Coleman, Robert E. "The Navigators . . . Fall Conference—
Discipleship Library." http://discipleshiplibrary.com/
pdfs/APP00059.pdf

Cooper, Barry. "The Greatest Challenge in Discipleship
Today." *Desiring God,* September 17, 2019.
https://www.desiringgod.org/articles/
the-greatest-challenge-in-discipleship-today

Copeland, Adam J. "Why Lead? Discipleship as
    Leadership." *The Christian Century* 130, no. 23 (2013):
    11–12.

Creswell, John W., and Cheryl N. Poth. 2018. *Qualitative Inquiry
    and Research Design: Choosing among Five Approaches*. Los
    Angeles, CA: Sage.

Creswell, John W., and J. David Creswell. 2018. *Research Design:
    Qualitative, Quantitative, and Mixed Methods Approaches*.
    Los Angeles, CA: Sage.

Critchley, Dale. "Rediscovering Disciple Making." *Missio
    Apostolica* 23, no. 2 (2015): 344–45.

Davis, Ben. "What Are the Assumptions of a
    Research Study?" Mvorganizing.org. June
    1, 2021. https://www.mvorganizing.org/
    what-are-the-assumptions-of-a-research-study

Dever, Mark. *To Lead Others, Become a Disciple.* Wheaton, IL:
    Crossway, 2019. https://www.crossway.org/articles/
    to-lead-others-become-a-disciple

DeYoung, Kevin, and Greg Gilbert. *What Is the Mission of the
    Church?: Making Sense of Social Justice, Shalom, and the
    Great Commission.* Wheaton, IL: Crossway, 2011.

Dollarhide, Maya. "Social Media Definition." *Investopedia*,
    August 31, 2021. https://www.investopedia.com/
    terms/s/social-media.asp.

Dooley, Larry M. "Case Study Research and Theory
          Building." *Sage Journals* 4, no. 3 (August 2002):
          335–354.

Dunaetz, David R. "Evangelism, Social Media, and the Mum
          Effect." *Evangelical Review of Theology* 43, no. 2 (2019):
          138–151.

Earley, Dave, and David Wheeler. *Evangelism Is . . . How to Share
          Jesus with Passion and Confidence*. Nashville, TN.: B & H
          Academic, 2010.

"Evangelism—Sharing the Gospel at Work
          (Overview)." Theology of Work. https://
          www.theologyofwork.org/key-topics/
          evangelism-sharing-the-gospel-at-work-overview

"Evangelism vs. Disciple Making: Joshua Project." *Joshua
          Project.* 2019. https://joshuaproject.net/resources/
          articles/evangelism_vs_disciple_making

Evangelista, Sam Reyes. "Developing a Contextual Cross-
          Cultural Evangelism and Church Growth Strategy for
          the International Bible Church, Hampton, Georgia."
          Boyce Digital Repository Home, May 30, 2013. https://
          repository.sbts.edu/handle/10392/4281

Everts, Don. *Go and Do: Becoming a Missional Christian.* Downers
          Grove, IL: IVP Books, 2012.

Focus on the Family. "Understanding the Meaning of
the Word 'Evangelical.'" January 7, 2021.
https://www.focusonthefamily.com/family-qa/
understanding-the-meaning-of-the-word-evangelical

Freeman, Tim. "How People Group Information Impacted a
Mission Agency." *Mission Frontiers*. http://www.mis-
sionfrontiers.org/issue/article/how-people-group-in-
formation-impacted-a-mission-agency

Gale. "'Immigration.' Opposing Viewpoints Online
Collection." Gale, a Cengage Company, 2018.
https://www.gale.com/open-access/immigration.

Gallardo, Luis Hassan, and Jeanne Batalova. "Filipino
Immigrants in the United States." Migrationpolicy.
org. https://www.migrationpolicy.org/article/
filipino-immigrants-united-states-2020

Ghazaryan Drissi, Ani. 2019. "What Is Transforming
Discipleship?" *Ecumenical Review* 71, no. 1/2 (2019):
216–24. http://doi.org/10.1111/erev.12421

Gorospe, Athena E. "Lausanne Occasional Paper: Case Study:
Overseas Filipino Workers." Lausanne Movement,
September 1, 2021. https://lausanne.org/content/
lop/case-study-overseas-filipino-workers-lop-62-g.

Gunnell, Martin. "Research Methodologies: A Comparison of Quantitative, Qualitative and Mixed Methods." LinkedIn, December 16, 2016. https://www.linkedin.com/pulse/research-methodologies-comparison-quantitative-mixed-methods-gunnell.

Hancock, Dawson R., and Robert Algozzine. *Doing Case Study Research: A Practical Guide for Beginning Researchers.* New York: Teachers College Press, 2017.

Hewitt, Roderick R. "Evangelism as Discipleship: Implications for Theological Education and Leadership Formation." *International Review of Mission* 103, no. 2 (2014): 200–214.

Honeycutt, Frank G. "Keep Jesus Weird: Discipleship Isn't Supposed to Be Easy." *The Christian Century* 132, no. 15 (2015): 10–11.

Huang, Josie. "Asian American, Christian, Progressive and Lonely. Is There a Church for You?" LAist. https://laist.com/2019/05/09/asian_american_christian_progressive_church.php

"'Immigration.' Opposing Viewpoints Online Collection, Gale, 2018." https://www.gale.com/open-access/immigration#immigration-more-articles.

International Organization for Migration. Country Migration
      Report: The Philippines 2013. https://www.cfo.gov.
      ph/publications/documents-on-migration-and-de-
      velopment/861-country-migration-report-the-philip-
      pines-2013.html

Irwin, Tim. *Impact: Great Leadership Changes Everything.* Dallas,
      TX: BenBella Books, 2014.

Jackson, Griffin Paul. "The Top Reasons Young People Drop
      Out of Church." *Christianity Today,* January 16, 2019.
      https://www.christianitytoday.com/news/2019/
      january/church-drop-out-college-young-adults-hia-
      tus-lifeway-survey.html

Kell, Garrett. "Discipleship According to the Scriptures."
      9Marks, August 27, 2012. https://www.9marks.org/
      article/journaldiscipleship-according-scriptures

Khan, Zakeer Ahmed, Allah Nawaz, and Irfanullah Khan.
      "Leadership Theories and Styles:
      A Literature Review." *Journal of Resources Development
      and Management* 16 (2016):
      1–7.

Kim, Billy. "The Motives for Evangelism." *The Mission of an
      Evangelist: Amsterdam 2000; A Conference of Preaching
      Evangelists.* Minneapolis, MN: Worldwide Publishers,
      2001.

Knoetze, Johannes J. "Who Are the Disciples? Identity
Perceptions about Millennials and the
Church." *Verbum et Ecclesia* 38, no. 1 (2017). http://
doi.org/10.4102/ve.v38i1.1718

Linneberg, Mai S., and Steffen Korsgaard. "(PDF) Coding
Qualitative Data: A Synthesis Guiding the Novice."
ResearchGate. https://www.researchgate.net/publi-
cation/332957319_Coding_qualitative_data_a_syn-
thesis_guiding_the_novice

MacArthur, John. *Evangelism: How to Share the Gospel Faithfully.*
The John MacArthur Pastors' Library. Nashville, TN:
Thomas Nelson, 2011.

Markham, Ian. "Introduction to Samuel M. Shoemaker,
'Church Congress Syllabus 47: Personal
Evangelism.'" *Anglican Theological Review* 100, no. 3
(2018): 479–80.

Marshall, Catherine, and Gretchen B. Rossman. 2016.
Designing Qualitative Research. Thousand Oaks, CA.:
Sage.

McClure, Paul K. "Faith and Facebook in a Pluralistic Age:
The Effects of Social Networking Sites on the
Religious Beliefs of Emerging Adults." *Sociological
Perspectives* 59, no. 4 (2016): 818-834.

Mitchell, Christopher W. "C.S. Lewis on Authentic
    Discipleship." C.S. Lewis Institute,
    2011. https://www.cslewisinstitute.org/
    CS_Lewis_on_Authentic_Discipleship_SinglePage

Moreau, A. Scott, Gary Corwin, and Gary B. McGee.
    Introducing World Missions Biblical, Historical, and Practical
    Survey. 2nd ed. Grand Rapids, MI: Baker Academic,
    2015.

National Association of Evangelicals. "What Is
    an Evangelical?" https://www.nae.org/
    what-is-an-evangelical

Nel, Malan, and W.J. Schoeman. "Rediscovering
    'Disciplemaking' and the Role of Faith-
    Sharing." *HTS Teologiese Studies* 75, no. 4 (2019).
    http://doi.org/10.4102/hts.v75i4.5119

Northouse, Peter Guy. 2021. *Introduction to Leadership: Concepts*
    and Practice. Thousand Oaks, CA: Sage.

Packer, J.I. *Evangelism and the Sovereignty of God.* Downers Grove,
    IL: IVP Books, 2012.

Palinkas, Lawrence A., Sarah M. Horwitz, Carla A. Green, Jennifer P. Wisdom, Naihua Duan, and Kimberly Hoagwood. "Purposeful Sampling for Qualitative Data Collection and Analysis in Mixed Method Implementation Research." *Administration and Policy in Mental Health: US National Library of Medicine,* September 2015. https://www.ncbi.nlm.nih.gov/pmc/articles/PMC4012002

Palmer, B. "Evangelism: Sharing Your Faith." *Grace Communion International,* October 1, 2018. https://www.gci.org/articles/sharing-your-faith

Palmer, Cathryne, and Amanda Bolderston. "A Brief Introduction to Qualitative Research." *The Canadian Journal of Medical Radiation Technology* 37(1): 16–19. http://doi.org/10.1016/S0820-5930(09)60112-2

Parks, Bryan. "Six Benefits of Evangelism for Discipleship." 9Marks, August 27, 2012. https://www.9marks.org/article/journalsix-benefits-evangelism-discipleship

Pew Research Center's Religion and Public Life Project. "Asian Americans: A Mosaic of Faiths." March 19, 2014. https://www.pewforum.org/2012/07/19/asian-americans-a-mosaic-of-faiths-overview

Piper, John. "Missions Exists Because Worship Doesn't." *Desiring God,* October 7, 2012. https://www.desiringgod.org/messages/missions-exists-because-worship-doesnt-a-bethlehem-legacy-inherited-and-bequeathed

Rachmawati, Ani Wahyu, and Donald C. Lantu. "Servant
Leadership Theory Development & Measurement."
Procedia—Social and Behavioral Sciences 115 (February
2014): 387–393. https://core.ac.uk/download/
pdf/81169095.pdf

Raga, Steven. "Intergenerational, Multiethnic, and
Transnational Approaches to US to US
Policy Advocacy for the Filipino American
Community. *Asian American Policy Review* 29 (2019):
30–38.

Rahman, Md Shidur. "The Advantages and Disadvantages
of Using Qualitative and Quantitative Approaches
and Methods in Language 'Testing and Assessment'
Research: A Literature Review." *Journal of Education
and Learning* 6, no. 1 (November 2016): 102–112.

Rashid, Yasir, Ammar Rashid, Muhammad Akib Warraich,
Sana Sameen Sabir, and Ansar Waseem.
"Case Study Method: A Step-by-Step Guide
for Business Researchers." *International Journal
of Qualitative Methods* 18 (2019). https://doi.
org/10.1177/1609406919862424

Roberts, Judith E. B. "Discipleship with the Marginalized at
the Centre." *International Review of Mission* 103, no. 2
(2014): 189–99.

Roces, Mina. "Filipina/o Migration to the United States and the Remaking of Gender Narratives, 1906-2010." *Gender & History* 27, no. 1 (2015): 190–206. http://doi.org/10.1111/1468-0424.12097

Salonen, Roxane B. "Come Follow Me." *US Catholic* 76, no. 7 (2011): 28.

Stiles, J. Mack. "How Should We Define Evangelism?" 9Marks. https://www.9marks.org/article/how-should-we-define-evangelism

Stoney, Sierra, and Jeanne Batalova. "Filipino Immigrants in the United States." *Migration Policy Institute*, June 5, 2013. https://www.immigrationresearch.org/system/files/Filipino%20Immigrants%20in%20the%20United%20States.pdf

Swindoll, Charles R. *Leadership: Influence That Inspires*. Waco, TX: Word Books, 1985.

Tabone, Eleanor. "Celebrating Filipino American History Month in South Carolina," October 13, 2021. https://www.google.com/amp/s/www.wltx.com/amp/article/news/community/filipino-american-history-month-sc/101-53423512-c046-47ae-a408-f32b98f5a670

Tan-Gatue, Peter. "Contextualizing Inductive Bible Study
(IBS) in a Postcolonial Filipino American Setting."
Asbury Theological Seminary, 2013. https://place.
asburyseminary.edu/cgi/viewcontent.cgi?refer-
er=&httpsredir=1&article=1187&context=asbury-
journal

Tawfik, Wedad A. "Discipleship Transforming the World: A
Coptic Orthodox Perspective." *International Review of
Mission* 106, no. 2 (2017): 268–79.

Terry, John Mark. *Missiology: An Introduction to the Foundations,
History, and Strategies of World Missions.* Nashville, TN:
B&H Academic, 2015.

Thomas, Gary. *How to Do Your Case Study: A Guide for Students and
Researchers.* Los Angeles, CA: Sage, 2016.

Tira, Sadiri Joy, and Enoch Wan. "The Filipino Experience
in Diaspora Missions: A Case Study of Christian
Communities in Contemporary Contexts." http://
www.edinburgh2010.org/fileadmin/files/edin-
burgh2010/files/Study_Process/EDINBURGH%20
COMMISSION%20VII%20tira%20diaspora.pdf.

Van Gelder, Craig, and Dwight J. Zscheile. *The Missional Church
in Perspective: Mapping Trends and Shaping the Conversation.*
Grand Rapids, MI: Baker Academic, 2011.

Vertovec, Steven. "The Political Importance of Diasporas."
migrationpolicy.org, June 1, 2005. https://www.
migrationpolicyinstitute-europe.com/article/
political-importance-diasporas

Vinson Jr., William Edward. "Is Southern Baptist Christianity
the Same as Christian Discipleship?" *Ethics & Critical
Thinking Journal* 2012, no. 3 (2012): 132–38.

"What Role Does Social Media Play in Your Faith Life?
America Readers Weigh In." *America Magazine*,
October 6, 2017. https://www.americamagazine.
org/faith/2017/10/05/what-role-does-social-media-
play-your-faith-life-america-readers-weigh

Williams, Andrew. "Re-Experiencing Evangelism in the
City." *International Review of Mission* 105, no. 1 (2016):
23–29.

Williams, Lara. "Let Faith Falter: So What If We Trust Social
Media Less and Less? That's a Good Thing, Says
Lara Williams." *New Scientist* 237 (2018): 24–25.

Wu, Jackson. *One Gospel for All Nations: A Practical Approach to
Biblical Contextualization.* Pasadena, CA: William Carey
Library, 2015.

Zong, Jie, and Jeanne Batalova. "Filipino Immigrants in the
United States." Migration Policy Institute, May 3,
2019. https://www.migrationpolicy.org/article/
filipino-immigrants-united-states

ENDNOTES

1   "Focus on the Family. "Understanding the Meaning of the Word 'Evangelical.'" January 7, 2021. https://www.focusonthefamily.com/family-qa/ understanding-the-meaning-of-the-word-evangelical

2   "Understanding the Meaning."

3   National Association of Evangelicals. "What Is an Evangelical?" https://www.nae.org/ what-is-an-evangelical

4   National Association of Evangelicals.

5   J. Mack Stiles. "How Should We Define Evangelism?" 9Marks. https://www.9marks.org/article/ how-should-we-define-evangelism

6   Stiles.

7   Andrew Williams. "Re-Experiencing Evangelism in the City." *International Review of Mission* 105, no. 1 (2016): 23–29. 29.

8   Ian Markham. "Introduction to Samuel M. Shoemaker, 'Church Congress Syllabus 47: Personal Evangelism.'" *Anglican Theological Review* 100, no. 3 (2018): 479–80.

9   Donald A. Carson. "Do the Work of an Evangelist." *Themelios* 39, no. 1 (2014): 1–4.

10   Carson. 2.

11   Andrew Williams. "Re-Experiencing Evangelism in the City." *International Review of Mission* 105, no. 1 (2016): 23–29; Williams also argues that church membership cannot be the primary aim of the proclamation of the

gospel and that there is no perfect set of words that capture the gospel. He adds that there are tensions about evangelism that need to be addressed. Finally, he argues that effective evangelism comes from the boldness to speak about the gospel and back it up with a lifestyle that honors the Lord.

[12] Billy Kim. "The Motives for Evangelism." *The Mission of an Evangelist: Amsterdam 2000; A Conference of Preaching Evangelists*. Minneapolis, MN: Worldwide Publishers, 2001. 15.

[13] George Carey. 2001. "Preaching Christ in a Broken World." *The Mission of an Evangelist: Amsterdam 2000; A Conference of Preaching Evangelists*. Minneapolis, MN: Worldwide Publishers. 89.

[14] Dave Earley and David Wheeler. 2010. *Evangelism Is . . . How to Share Jesus with Passion and Confidence*. Nashville, TN: B & H Academic. 184.

[15] Early and Wheeler. 184.

[16] Packer, J.I. *Evangelism and the Sovereignty of God*. Downers Grove, IL: IVP Books, 2012. 45.

[17] "Evangelism—Sharing the Gospel at Work (Overview)." Theology of Work. https://www.theologyofwork.org/key-topics/evangelism-sharing-the-gospel-at-work-overview.

[18] "Evangelism."

[19] B. Palmer. "Evangelism: Sharing Your Faith." *Grace Communion International*, October 1, 2018. https://www.gci.org/articles/sharing-your-faith

[20] Jeremy Bourna. "What Is Evangelism?" *Zondervan Academic*. https://zondervanacademic.com/blog/evangelism

21 Although there may be cultural overlap, this study
    will not focus on other Asian immigrants. This work is
    delimited to understanding the day-to-day lives of these
    immigrants in their newfound culture and how evange-
    lism could change their lifestyles. Regarding evangelism,
    the scope of the study is delimited to an evangelical
    understanding of the term and not the definitions found
    in other traditions.

    This study was an attempt to develop an evangelism strat-
    egy for Filipino immigrants in Columbia, South Carolina.
    It may be used as a precedent for future research that
    focuses on evangelizing Filipino immigrants in the United
    States and other parts of the world. Moreover, this study
    will be a good addition to existing cross-cultural research
    about evangelizing different ethnic groups.

22 Luis Hassan Gallardo and Jeanne Batalova. "Filipino
    Immigrants in the United States." migrationpolicy.org,
    May 17, 2021. https://www.migrationpolicy.org/article/
    filipino-immigrants-united-states-2020

23 Sierra Stoney and Jeanne Batalova. "Filipino Immigrants
    in the United States." *Migration Policy Institute*, June 5,
    2013. https://www.immigrationresearch.org/system/
    files/Filipino%20Immigrants%20in%20the%20
    United%20States.pdf

24 Tan-Gatue, Peter. "Contextualizing Inductive Bible Study
    (IBS) in a Postcolonial Filipino American Setting." Asbury
    Theological Seminary, 2013. https://place.asburysemi-
    nary.edu/cgi/viewcontent.cgi?referer=&httpsredir=1&ar-
    ticle=1187&context=asburyjournal. 77.

25 Bryan Parks. "Six Benefits of Evangelism
    for Discipleship." 9Marks, August 27,
    2012. https://www.9marks.org/article/

journalsix-benefits-evangelism-discipleship

26   Tabone, Eleanor. "Celebrating Filipino American History Month in South Carolina," October 13, 2021. https://www.google.com/amp/s/www.wltx.com/amp/article/news/community/filipino-american-history-month-sc/101-53423512-c046-47ae-a408-f32b98f5a670

27   Another important aspect of evangelism that every believer should understand concerns motives. According to Packer, two motives should come to every believer's mind when doing evangelism. First, the motive to glorify God, which is the chief end of man. The author presented many Scriptures from the New Testament that clearly demonstrated that obedience to God's commandments brings glory to Him. He added that "men glorify God by obeying His word and fulfilling his revealed will" (74.) Second, every believer should have the motive of love for neighbor, and the desire to see fellow humans saved. According to Packer, "the wish to win the lost for Christ should be, and indeed is, the natural, spontaneous outflow of love in the heart of everyone who has been born again" (76).

28   Packer. 74.

29   Packer. 76.

30   Pew Research Center's Religion and Public Life Project. "Asian Americans: A Mosaic of Faiths." March 19, 2014. https://www.pewforum.org/2012/07/19/asian-americans-a-mosaic-of-faiths-overview

31   Mike Barnett and Robin Martin. 2012. *Discovering the Mission of God: Best Missional Practices for the 21st Century.* Downers Grove, IL: IVP Academic, 2012. 19.

32   Eddie Arthur. "Missio Dei and the Mission of the

Church." Wycliffe Global Alliance. https://www.wycliffe. net/more-about-what-we-do/papers-and-articles/ missio-dei-and-the-mission-of-the-church

[33] Eddie Arthur.

[34] Barnett and Martin. 18–19.

[35] John Mark Terry. 2015. *Missiology: An Introduction to the Foundations, History, and Strategies of World Missions.* Nashville, Tennessee: B&H Academic. 10–13. Steve Addison, an author, speaker, and catalyst for movements that multiply disciples and churches, encourages Christians to actively get into missionary movements started by the Lord Jesus Christ. According to the author, "Jesus was the first missionary. He didn't start an organization, he didn't write a book, and he didn't run for office. What Jesus did was to found a missionary movement that would one day span the globe" (29). The author stresses that "His mission was to seek and to save them by giving his life as a ransom for them" (29).

[36] Steve Addison. *Movements That Change the World: Five Keys to Spreading the Gospel.* Rev. ed. Downers Grove, Ill: IVP Books, 2011. 32.

[37] Tim Freeman. "How People Group Information Impacted a Mission Agency." *Mission Frontiers.* http:// www.missionfrontiers.org/issue/article/how-people-group-information-impacted-a-mission-agency

[38] Kevin DeYoung and Greg Gilbert. 2011. *What Is the Mission of the Church?: Making Sense of Social Justice, Shalom, and the Great Commission.* Wheaton, IL: Crossway. 41–43.

[39] *What Is the Mission?* 180.

[40] Piper, John. "Missions Exists Because Worship Doesn't." *Desiring God,* October 7, 2012. https://www.

desiringgod.org/messages/missions-exists-because-worship-doesnt-a-bethlehem-legacy-inherited-and-bequeathed

[41] Arthur clarified that Missio Dei is a Latin theological term that can be translated as "Mission of God." It is understood that Missio Dei "refers to the work of the church as being part of God's work. So the church's mission is a subset of a larger whole mission that is it is both part of God's mission to the world and not the entirety of God's work in the world." Missio Dei and the church should come together to bring change in the lives of people in communities. However, they clarified that it is the mission of God that ought to fuel the church for mission work. It is written, "Missio Dei brings a correction to this view by putting God, not the church or denomination, at the centre of mission. Mission is the originator of the Church, not the other way round."

[42] Steven Vertovec. "The Political Importance of Diasporas." migrationpolicy.org, June 1, 2005. https://www.migrationpolicyinstitute-europe.com/article/political-importance-diasporas.

[43] Roces, Mina. "Filipina/o Migration to the United States and the Remaking of Gender Narratives, 1906-2010." *Gender & History* 27, no. 1 (2015): 190–206. http://doi.org/10.1111/1468-0424.12097.190.

[44] Tan-Gatue. 77.

[45] Josie Huang. "Asian American, Christian, Progressive And Lonely. Is There a Church for You?" *LAist.* https://laist.com/2019/05/09/asian_american_christian_progressive_church.php.

[46] John W. Creswell and J. David Creswell. *Research Design:*

Qualitative, Quantitative, and Mixed Methods Approaches. Los Angeles, CA: Sage, 2018. 4.

47   John W. Creswell and Cheryl N. Poth. 2018. *Qualitative Inquiry and Research Design: Choosing among Five Approaches*. Los Angeles, CA: Sage, 2018. 6.

48   Cathryne Palmer and Amanda Bolderston. "A Brief Introduction to Qualitative Research." *The Canadian Journal of Medical Radiation Technology* 1: 16–19. http://doi.org/10.1016/S0820-5930(09)60112-2

49   Rahman, Md Shidur. "The Advantages and Disadvantages of Using Qualitative and Quantitative Approaches and Methods in Language 'Testing and Assessment' Research: A Literature Review." *Journal of Education and Learning* 6, no. 1 (November 2016): 102–112. "Firstly, the qualitative research approach produces the thick (detailed) description of participants' feelings, opinions, and experiences; . . . Secondly, qualitative research approach (interpretivism) holistically understands the human experience in specific settings. . . . Thirdly, interpretivism research approach is regarded as ideographic research, . . . Fourthly, the qualitative research admits Is to discover the participants' inner experience, and to figure out how meanings are shaped through and in culture. . . . Fifthly, qualitative research methods such as participant-observation, unstructured interviews, direct observation, describing records are most commonly used for collecting data. . . . and sixthly, qualitative research design (interactive approach) has a flexible structure as the design can be constructed and reconstructed to a greater extent."

50   Creswell and Poth. 16.

51   Creswell and Poth. 16–18.

52 Creswell and Poth. 19.

53 Creswell and Poth. 21.

54 Ani Wahyu Rachmawati and Donald C. Lantu. "Servant Leadership Theory Development & Measurement." *Procedia—Social and Behavioral Sciences* 115 (February 2014): 387–393. https://core.ac.uk/download/pdf/81169095. pdf. 388.

55 Mark Dever. *To Lead Others, Become a Disciple.* Wheaton, IL: Crossway, 2019. https://www.crossway.org/articles/to-lead-others-become-a-disciple

56 Garrett Kell. "Discipleship According to the Scriptures." 9Marks, August 27, 2012.

57 Ani Ghazaryan Drissi. "What Is Transforming Discipleship?" *Ecumenical Review* 71, no. 1/2 (2019): 216–24. http://doi.org/10.1111/erev.12421

58 Barry Cooper. "The Greatest Challenge in Discipleship Today." *Desiring God,* September 17, 2019. https://www.desiringgod.org/articles/the-greatest-challenge-in-discipleship-today

59 I was directed here by Christopher W. Mitchell. "C.S. Lewis on Authentic Discipleship." C.S. Lewis Institute, 2011. https://www.cslewisinstitute.org/CS_Lewis_on_Authentic_Discipleship_SinglePage.

60 Mitchell.

61 Mitchell.

62 Adam J. Copeland, "Why Lead? Discipleship as Leadership." *The Christian Century* 130, no. 23 (2013): 11–12.

    Roderick R. Hewitt. "Evangelism as Discipleship: Implications for Theological Education and Leadership

Formation." *International Review of Mission* 103, no. 2 (2014): 200–214. Hewitt challenged our perceptions of who should disciple. For instance, some churches rely solely on the pastor to disciple Christians. Hewitt considered the impact of theological education in Jamaica. He pointed out that although the country suffers from a high crime rate and unemployment, more churches are arising. He suggested that although it is true that the goal of evangelism is to increase church membership and make churches self-sufficient, there is a danger in putting too much emphasis on having those with theological education lead the church. It was incorrect for church members to rely solely on their leaders to do the works of the ministry instead of becoming participants in church evangelism and discipleship. I felt challenged to make sure that all church members are given the opportunity to exercise their God-given talents to edify the body of Christ.

Wedad A. Tawfik. "Discipleship Transforming the World: A Coptic Orthodox Perspective." International Review of Mission 106, no. 2 (2017): 268–79. Tawfik argues that the core of Christianity is based on the work of the Holy Spirit and that the Christian response to the Great Commission is discipleship. Tawfik claims that there will be no discipleship without the Holy Spirit who give gifts to those who teach and evangelize. He adds that the church plays a vital role in making disciples for Christ. He shares about the Coptic Orthodox commitment to the Great Commission through education and monasticism. Tawfik contends that if Christians will not acknowledge the Holy Spirit in the process of making disciples, then the church discipleship is a mere program and not a ministry of the Holy Spirit.

Honeycutt, Frank G. "Keep Jesus Weird: Discipleship Isn't Supposed to Be Easy." *The Christian Century* 132, no. 15 (2015): 10–11. Honeycutt states that the most painful thing a pastor experiences is when a prospective church member decides to leave the church. Honeycutt insists that discipleship is not supposed to be easy. He comments on Nicodemus's encounter with Jesus and how Nicodemus became a true follower of Christ. He challenges pastors, evangelists, and missionaries to avoid sugar coating the preaching of the gospel to please people and become a part of the church. In contrast, he argues that true conversion involves strict training and study of the Scripture. He adds that Christians should not take discipleship lightly but consider it the serious business of Christ (Honeycutt 2015).

Nel, Malan, and W.J. Schoeman. "Rediscovering 'Disciplemaking' and the Role of Faith-Sharing." *HTS Teologiese Studies* 75, no. 4 (2019). http://doi.org/10.4102/hts.v75i4.5119 Malan and Schoeman discuss discipleship and found it "is about the intentional training of people who voluntarily submit to the Lordship of Christ and who want to become imitators of Him in every thought, word, and deed" (3). "Discipling is what we do any way as we live life and while we learn how to live life to its fullest, as Jesus gives it" (3).

Roberts, Judith E. B. "Discipleship with the Marginalized at the Centre." *International Review of Mission* 103, no. 2 (2014): 189–99. Roberts clarifies that as followers of Christ, our mandate is to go beyond our comfort zones and make disciples for Christ. Roberts argues that "as disciples of Christ, together we are sent into the world, for the sake of the world that we may be transformed by the Word" (189). The Lord calls us to be in a mission, and our mission is to care for those who are hurting. She summarized that the marginalized are those who are lonely, oppressed, poor, hungry, imprisoned, angry and suffering in mind, body, or spirit. Roberts challenges Christians to remember that discipleship is for all levels of people regardless of their physical, emotional, and spiritual condition (89).

Dever defined being a disciple as deliberately doing something good for someone so that they will become like Christ in the process. Before a person can make a disciple, they must first become a disciple. He clarifies that "being a disciple of Christ, in other words does not begin with something we do. It begins with something Christ did." As for discipleship, the author contended that "our discipleship to Christ begins when we hear those two words and obey them: 'Follow me.'"

63 Dever.

64 Carr, Caleb T., and Rebecca Hayes. "Social Media: Defining, Developing, and Divining." *Atlantic Journal of Communication* 23, no. 1 (2015):46–65. https://doi. org/http://doi.org/ 10.1080/15456870.2015.972282: "Social media are Internet-based channels that allow users to opportunistically interact and selectively self-present, either in real-time or asynchronously, with both broad and narrow audiences who derive value from user-generated content and the perception of interaction with others" (8). Moreover, the authors explained what they mean by Internet-based as follows: "The Internet refers to the interconnected computer networks across the globe and refers predominantly to the system infrastructure; while the World Wide Web is one of many applications using the Internet's infrastructure to communicate

through audiovisual hyperlinks and accessed through a browser" (9).

[65] David R. Dunaetz. "Evangelism, Social Media, and the Mum Effect." *Evangelical Review of Theology* 43, no. 2 (2019): 138–151. 143.

[66] Lara Williams. "Let Faith Falter: So What If We Trust Social Media Less and Less? That's a Good Thing, Says Lara Williams." *New Scientist* 237 (2018): 24–25.

[67] Nadeem Badshah. "Thou Shall Not Commit Social Media Offenses: Faith Groups Back Church of England's Digital Charter." *Eastern Eye*, July 19, 2019.

[68] MacClure 2016, 818. "Faith and Facebook in a Pluralistic Age: The Effects of Social

Networking Sites on the Religious Beliefs of Emerging Adults." *Sociological Perspectives* 59, no. 4 (2016): 818.

[69] Roxane B. Salonen. "Come Follow Me." *US Catholic* 76, no. 7 (2011): 28. 28.

[70] Consent forms for this research were obtained from Columbia International University's Institutional Review Board. These forms were used to obtain permission from the participants to take part in the interviews. I gave the form to the interviewees, asking them to read the form. After they have read the form, he asked the participants if they have any questions regarding the consent form. When the participants agreed to the conditions, I asked the participants to sign the consent form. Before conducting the interview, I read the disclaimer to the participants.

[71] To better understand the information gathered during the interviews, it is helpful to know how long the participants have resided in the United States. Column 2 of this table shows the number of years that the immigrants

has been living in the US. The third column indicates the languages and dialects that the immigrants speak. Understanding the immigrants' dialect will guide the church to effectively reach out to them with the gospel using their own dialects.

[72] The data in this research were gathered through interviews and participant observations. The first step in the process was to obtain a consent form from Columbia International University's Institutional Research Board. After obtaining the form from the IRB, I sent an invitation to Filipino immigrants in Columbia, South Carolina, to participate in the study. The invitation was sent through text messages and through Facebook messenger.

[73] After the participants accepted the invitation, an appointment was scheduled to meet face-to-face with each participant. I began each interview by explaining the purpose of the study. The participants then were asked to sign a written consent.

[74] I collected data by recording all the interview sessions using open-ended questions. While recording, I took notes to make sure that important information will not be missed. Before I analyzed the data, I transcribed all interviews using a software program called Otter.ai. I then sent a copy of the transcription to participants to review along with a Participant Member-Checking Form. I have created Microsoft Word files for all transcribed interviews, field notes, and participant observations. All files were saved and password-protected in my personal laptop computer so that I have the only access.

In this research, an ethical framework for gathering the data was carefully observed. I ensured that the identities of all participants in this study are protected using codes in place of names. In the process of transcribing the re-corded interview, I used codes such as P1 for participant number 1 and P2 for participant number 2. The original transcriptions bear the names of the participants and is stored in my personal filing cabinet for safekeeping. I will keep the transcriptions for a year before they will be shredded. Before conducting the research interviews and data collection, I applied for IRB full board review at Columbia International University's International Research Board. The approval was obtained on April 19, 2021, under the rules for expedited review. I believed that obtaining the approval from IRB will ensure the protec-tion of the participants.

[75] Creswell and Poth. 165–166.

[76] Creswell and Creswell. 93–94.

[77] Before the face-to-face interviews, participants were notified orally and in writing about the purpose of the study as well as the collection of the data, analysis, and the methods of storing the data of the research study. I discussed with the participants their rights to withdraw at any time from their participation in this study as well as their rights to review the written transcript of their interview and make corrections. The participants were also informed that the data collected in this research will be stored in my house for safekeeping. The participants' rights were carefully observed, and they were informed about their ownership of their portion of the research.

[78] Mai S. Linneberg and Steffen Korsgaard. "(PDF) Coding Qualitative Data: A Synthesis Guiding the Novice." ResearchGate. https://www.researchgate.net/publica-tion/332957319_Coding_qualitative_data_a_synthesis_guiding_the_novice. The authors state that "an important

tool in the process of turning raw qualitative data into a communicative and trustworthy 'story' is coding" (3). The authors add that "coding in its most basic form is the simple operation of identifying segments of meaning in your data and labelling them with a code, which can be defined as 'a word or short phrase that symbolically assigns a summative, salient, essence-capturing, and/ or evocative attribute for a portion of language-based or visual data'" (6). The authors shared the advantages of coding: "(1) Acquire deep, comprehensive, and thorough insights into your data . . . (2) Make the data easily accessible and retrievable . . . (3) Sort and structure your data . . . (4) Ensuring transparency . . . (5) Ensuring validity . . . and (6) giving a voice to one's participants" (7–9).

[79] I want first to address the focus of the first research questions I listed above, namely the basic understanding of Christianity among Filipino immigrants. The recorded interviews conducted with seventeen participants resulted in 97 pages of data using Otter.ai for transcription. After transcribing, I carefully analyzed each transcription and checked the recordings for confirmation of the accuracy of the data. Because the participants are immigrants and spoke in their second language, the software did not always accurately transcribe the information. I made appropriate edits to ensure the transcription was accurate. After verification, I sent a copy of the appropriate transcript to each participant to validate the accuracy of their answers to the interview questions. After the participants reviewed the transcript, I asked each participant to sign the participant member-checking form. During this process, there were only minor corrections that were made.

I analyzed and edited the interview transcripts. The next step was to conduct the manual coding using Microsoft

Word. I read every transcript and noted every word or phrase that I believed to be relevant for the study.

[80] Interview with Lorna, November 29, 2021.

[81] Interview of Isabel, November 23, 2021

[82] Interview with Tess, November 17, 2021.

[83] Interview with Robert, November 23, 2021.

[84] Interview with Alma, November 29, 2021.

[85] Interview with Randy, November 11, 2021.

[86] Interview with Rudy, November 29, 2021

[87] Interview with George, November 11, 2021.

[88] Interview with Renato, November 29, 2021.

[89] Roces. 190.

CPSIA information can be obtained
at www.ICGtesting.com
Printed in the USA
BVHW050538220623
666248BV00016B/208